SEX AND THE NOW GENERATION

SEX
AND
THE
NOW
GENERATION

SCOTT N. JONES

JOHN KNOX PRESS
Richmond, Virginia

International Standard Book Number: 0-8042-2169-3
Library of Congress Catalog Card Number: 73-107324
© M. E. Bratcher 1970
Printed in the United States of America

To my wife,
MARTHA,
and
to a decade of college students
who have so enriched
our lives

CONTENTS

Contents 9

SEX
AND THE
NOW
GENERATION

---- ◖▷ ----

INTRODUCTION

Janice sits on the bed talking to her roommate. A little tear tries to edge its way over her eyelid. "I wanted him desperately to make love to me, and now I wonder why. I don't think I really wanted him. I just wanted to be loved, and have someone prove that I was lovable. Now I simply hate myself!"

Eric and Marge are in their clergyman's office. Eric's gestures indicate their confusion. "There must be a reasonable answer to this. Marge and I have been going together seriously for a year and a half. We're engaged to be married, but that's several months away still. We know we're in love. Why must we wait until marriage to make love? Frankly, Parson, we've just about had it, and we don't know if we should, or can, wait."

Bruce shifts on the bar stool, and orders another beer. Thinking about the girl he has dated for a few times, he says to himself: "She really is a fine gal . . . I think. With some of them it's hard to tell; we're all playing games, jockeying for position. God, I get tired of that! But it's worse to be found out; if we guys don't put on the right image the gals don't take it up. If Betsy really knew what I was like . . . it might just be safer to go back to bed-hopping. That doesn't give any one of them a chance to know me too well."

Carolyn is confiding in her older sister: "I had to know what it was like. It's been so terribly hard to keep my emotions under control. I'd get excited and couldn't think of anything but the sheer bliss of going the whole way. I was so disappointed, Sis, that I cried for the next two days solid. Why was it so disappointing? What's wrong with me?"

Cliff is talking to his pledge son, and he is serious: "It's not all it's cracked up to be. Sure, there's a quick thrill, but you have to go to so many troubles and preliminaries to get to it. Cool off!"

Sally, after much brooding, has come at last to her housemother. She has to talk to someone and Mrs. Thrash seems so open and understanding. And Sally needs to understand some things much more clearly. Being a freshman is a lot harder than she anticipated.

She explains to Mrs. Thrash that her mother sat her down before she left for school, and that they had a long talk on the importance and virtues of remaining sexually chaste throughout college. Of course, Mother did most of the talking, but what she said seemed sensible enough. Then, Sally relates, Mother came to the crux of the matter. "Sally, it is by far the best not to go 'all the way' until you're married. But Sally, dear, things have changed so and there are so many temptations. Well, ah, I want you to take these pills to school with you, ah, just in case. If you *must* go, um, 'all the way,' do, for God's sake, start these beforehand."

Sally expresses to Mrs. Thrash what was at first her confusion, then her anger. "I get here on campus, and 'the pill' is all over the place. They must ship them in by the carload. Almost anyone can get them easily from one source or another, and they do! If the pill is effective in preventing pregnancy, and it obviously is, what's the big scare about possibly getting pregnant anymore? Remaining chaste has lost one of its biggest props. But what makes me angry is that after all of Mother's fine, sensible talk, she is saying to me by giving me the pills that finally she does not trust me. That hurt and I'm plenty mad!"

Bert has been nervous all evening, and when his mother finally leaves the room, he starts pacing the floor and finally blurts out: "Dad, I have to tell you something . . . something important . . . something that's going to mess up everything . . . I'm in trouble . . . that is . . . Oh, God . . . Joany is in trouble . . . She's pregnant, Dad!"

Some of our young people get so confused about their sexual needs and behavior that they are sometimes tempted "to take a pass" on the whole matter. There is too little help from their parents—they too do not feel confident in the way they handle the whole touchy subject. The churches also grope for relevance; historically they have a basic position about sexual practice before marriage and several codes of conduct, but they recognize that much of the latter is no longer subscribed to. The school system can and often does give sound clinical data about the sexual processes, but in most cases it does not assume the responsibility of teaching values related to sex.

Janice, and Bruce, and the rest of them are left in a no man's land where the only thing larger than their sexual appetite is their sexual confusion. To these young people in the late teens and early twenties, the old mores no longer are operative. They consider a Puritan ethic strictly out of the question; it is harsh and unreasonable and against anything and everything that might be fun. The Puritanistic ethics concerning sexual behavior are not even up for their consideration; they have been consciously and categorically discarded.

And today's young people, a good many of them, have gone one step further. Permissiveness has taken the place of morality. Sexual behavior is seldom approached any longer as a moral or an immoral issue. Sex is something to be practical about; it is there for the using. They have lived and breathed an atmosphere of permissiveness, and readily apply it to their sexual conduct.

But as with Bert or Carolyn, often the consequences turn out badly. Their sexual engagements boomerang on them and cause a razor-edged disappointment to themselves and to their families. Bert's father would prefer a heart attack to the words he has just heard from his son. Painful disillusionment surrounds Carolyn in her bewildering disappointment about her first sex experience. And Eric and Marge are, it would seem, hopelessly caught between desire and control.

From all of this, sex is seen as a great power or appetite that leads more to frustration than fulfillment. It would seem, at least, that sexual experiences leave more debris—the crowd of the sexually disillusioned—than they do bliss. Certainly the sexual drive is one of the strongest ones we know. It can take us to the "heights and depths." But for the human species it is not automatic or magical. It can be the source or the expression of unconditional joy and fulfillment or of intense anxiety and pain. Sex for human beings knows no neutral ground. We are not saying that the only thing sex causes is complications and troubles. Sex can be one of the most powerful, wonderful forces that is ours to have and to share; not simply because it is here but because of how it is used.

Therefore, this book purposes to celebrate sex. It intends to explore its meanings and possibilities, and to do so for young people. Our approach is positive, not negative. It seeks to be sane and sensible. It explores the current situation and examines the background for it. More importantly, it seeks to give strong and useful guidelines for meaningful sexual life and experience.

So let us then begin the celebration!

TAKING
A SERIOUS LOOK
AT SEX

---------------- 1 ----------------

Puritanism Passé

The strain and discomfort that plague Eric and Marge are not unusual ones. Here are two substantially mature young people. They are engaged to be married within a few months. Their relationship has grown and developed, and with it, greater physical attachment and affection. Their love as it has progressed has included a great deal of respect for one another as persons, and they are anticipating a life together filled with much joy and pleasure.

But they have been taught that sex belongs to marriage; that somehow being married suddenly makes sexual expression legitimate. More than that, they have come from families who have taken a Puritan or semi-Puritan approach to matters of sex: Sex is primarily for procreating children; we are not to take pleasure from it, for it is a naughty, trouble-making thing even sometimes within marriage, always so outside it. Such puritanical teaching in the past was, in practical terms, the most effective way to avoid premarital pregnancies. Sex is emotion; we must keep it under the strict control of the rational. The will must never allow itself to submit to the pleasures of the body. Sex is a second-class part of us, and we must keep it down! To cater to the flesh is to be taken in by the devil.

So sex ends up as our enemy, not our friend. Sex out-side marriage becomes dirty and nasty and a cardinal sin. Sex within marriage must be anticipated only for the sake of creating children. To be sure, this is an exaggerated inter-pretation of the Puritan outlook, but this code was often put into practice and these are the forms it took. Fathers and mothers instructed their children that sex was the great threat hanging over their heads. If they became sexually loose or promiscuous, they had done the most evil thing possible in the eyes of God.

Eric and Marge find this view, even in its recent liberali-zation, wholly unacceptable. They are serious about doing the right thing, but are equally serious in finding this puri-tanical outlook out of the question. They consider it narrow and negative, and simply to be abandoned, if for no other reason than it is no longer a powerful argument. With con-traceptives of all sorts readily available, they know they need not fear pregnancy. And they do not feel that sex is second-class and to be suppressed by a strong act of the will. They *do* feel that it is a good thing, and a central part of their lives. They feel that their sexual emotions are wholesome and to be enjoyed.

And as they reject the old sex ethic, they raise the ques-tion of the relationship between marriage and their physical and sexual behavior. We are in love now, they say, and in fact they are responsible about their love. Why does marriage suddenly make a full and wholesome sexual experience legiti-mate? Marriage does not make a relationship right; the two people do that. Why must the marriage ceremony give the only sanction for having sex? When we are in love, they con-tend, why can't we do the most natural thing and express it thoughtfully and sensibly to one another? Why should we wait? It puts on us an impossible and senseless—and un-necessary—strain!

Out of all of this, it becomes clear to us that the old sexual mores have broken down. They have been laid aside as no longer workable, even if they were right in the first place; but their rightness is rejected as well. Puritanism as such is gone; only here and there the hangover of Puritan ethics remains. Most of today's high school and college students would not even vaguely consider approaching their sexual conduct from these antique mores.

However, many of them want to approach the whole matter of sex with some sensible criterion, as do Eric and Marge. There will always be some who will treat the matter lightly and irresponsibly. They seek neither an old morality nor a new morality. No code would contain them. But there are many others who genuinely desire something positive and helpful. They are not wholly sure of themselves, nor of the meanings or the power of their sexual urges. They cannot accept the old morality, but they fail to see positive mores emerging on which they can depend. They are quite aware of the countless analyses made of our young, not least concerning sex. They are weary of the endless procession of labels attached to their particular generation, be it silent, jittery or whatever.

In any event, young people like Eric and Marge want to live out their lives as responsibly as they do passionately . . . both! They feel that sex has come out from under the sheets and is no longer encumbered by strict creeds of conduct. They feel that this is all to the good, that sexuality is now free to be measurably more meaningful. In short, they want a "high" view of sex, not a "low" one. It will be our purpose to attempt such a view at a later point.

A New Kind of World

Things do change as the times do, and assuredly our young people are in a period of great transition. The security and stability which marked the so-called Victorian Age have disappeared. Family life then was secure, disheveled for what they thought was a temporary period with the First World War. Generations of families generally stayed in the same part of the country, if not the same county. Father represented authority and gave a kind of dependable security to his own nest.

Then came the Great Depression of the Thirties, followed by a second global war, and a new era opened with new possibilities and new dangers. This adds a second dimension to that of the death of Puritan morality, and we must take it into full account if we are to understand both the problems and the demands of today's young people.

From the beginning of World War II there has been a serious and sharp dislocation of that earlier stability. The generations born during that war and since have lived in a different kind of world from their grandparents, and perhaps their own parents. During the war families were separated. If the father was not away fighting, he was working long and exhausting hours in the war effort. Near the end of the war the era of nuclear power was ushered in, and from that time on the world has been on edge in fear of its devastating use. Then the "cold war" came over the horizon, and the nations became more nervous.

All of this was the atmosphere in which post-war young people were raised; they have never known a period of stability and security. Their entire life spans thus far have been enfolded in tension; even the family unit has almost literally put on wheels as it has become more mobile than settled. They have always lived their lives on the verge of crisis, but, interestingly enough, have never experienced crises except those of an intensely personal sort like a death in the family or something of a similar nature. It is for this very reason perhaps that their primary orientation is so "personal-centered," whether dealing with sex, or marriage, or vocation, or religion, or morality, or war and peace or students' rights and freedoms. And this has important strengths, inasmuch as they are endeavoring to be persons rather than things on the population market. Its danger is that so often the interpersonal and social dimensions of living shrink out of perspective. Even when participating in groups or gangs or causes, everything finally centers on the self, and above all, the self-image.

Consider the compulsion of Bruce. He is not sure of his self-image, and therefore is inhibited in revealing himself to the girls he dates. Everything focuses on his awareness of how well or how poorly he is managing the image that he is trying painfully to create for others to see and accept.

The emphasis on self-image has given shape to the younger generation's concerns about sexual meaning and expression, as we shall see later more fully. Self-concern, added to the fact that they have never experienced any great degree of stability and security, only further complicates the matter of their sexual expression.

There is an additional factor which we must take into account if we are to take correctly the pulse of the needs and demands of young people. It is all summed up in the word *permissive*. Today's young people, and many of their parents for that matter, have fed on a steady diet of permissiveness. As the older standards disintegrated the popular practice was to do most anything that seemed not too dangerous or too silly! Through the popularization of John Dewey, permissiveness became a substitute code of practice as the old ways were disbanded.

Permissiveness has its place, but in filling up to overflowing the void left by Puritanism and Victorianism, it leaves young people struggling to keep their heads above its surface. Many fail to do so. We have paid a great price for our excessive permissiveness; and it seems that many young people would like to leave that too behind. Over-permissiveness results in a lack of realism. It causes our expectations—and therefore our motivations—to misjudge the facts. These times, as we shall see, require a frank realism, and assuredly cannot afford illusion. We must know who we are and what we are about, and live our lives out on that basis. And to measure the facts accurately will cause us to construct (or reconstruct) some practical and workable values, not least in the area of physical affection and sexual intercourse.

The "Sexual Revolution"

Much has been said about the current "sexual revolution," and there are popularizers of this idea, some for very dubious motivations. Certainly there is considerably more freedom in the discussion of sex and sexual practices than ever existed before World War II, and in most cases this is all to the good. Something as powerful and important as sex should not be hidden in a morass of the secretive and sinister.

But there is much more here than simply a sexual revolution which would seek to unshackle itself from former mores. A revolution, yes, but at the deepest level it is a moral revolution. What, really, makes a matter moral or immoral? We shall deal with this in full at a later point, but as applied to the so-called sexual revolution, the disillusionment of so many young people today seems to express itself in the sometimes harsh way they judge the moral-amoral-immoral conduct of their elders. Why, they complain, justifiably or not, do the adults of our world insist we have a sexual morality before marriage when so often they themselves have too little morality *within* their own marriages? Cannot some of our relationships, they contend, which are good and basically healthy be considered in fact more moral than some of the sexual abuses of those already married? Immorality is not limited, they know from their own observations, to the unmarried state.

It is little wonder then that so many young people approach premarital sexual relationships as strictly amoral, or at least without traditional moral criteria or consequences.

This is not to say however that they really want to abandon the moral questions. Rather they seek to dislodge themselves from the *form* of morality that has been handed down to them, as being no longer applicable or attainable. They deeply desire sensible standards of sexual behavior despite their disavowal of traditional American morality. They are no longer anxious to reexamine the old, but they are nevertheless eager to reconstruct some manner of orderly and meaningful sexual behavior: they are raising the basic moral questions by means of a new language and a new approach (which will be the concern of the following chapter). While this may be perplexing to their elders, even to causing them great anguish, the serious intent of the young people of today is to reexamine, radically if necessary, their lives and behavior in every conceivable respect. And this is where they begin: not with the past but with the present, not with the standards of an earlier day but with the existential concerns and problems of their own pulsing lives, not with consideration of the social implications of their conduct but with an intense focus on their persons . . . body, mind and soul.

"Sexed-Up Sex"

There is one further consideration in filling out this brief description of the current scene. It is the accusation made against the movie and TV industries and against certain forms of both serious and pulp literature of contributing to the breakdown of morality and principle. The charge is made that our young people are barraged by obscene and pornographic materials. All of this is largely true. There will always be those who will exploit the new advantage of a greater freedom of discussion about sexual matters.

However the suppression of such art forms and literature will not touch the central issue, as some look at and read these materials lightheartedly while others use them less healthfully. It makes a great deal of difference what the reader or viewer brings with him to these materials. This recalls Carolyn, the girl who so craved the "heights" that her fantasy world held out to her in sexual orgasm. She had pictured sexual fulfillment in exaggerated terms, intensified by what she had seen and read in popular sexual literature; but it is also significant that she *needed to exaggerate*. Remember, too, Bruce, who was so painfully concerned with his own self-image, whether or not he could "measure the man" and whether or not he could risk being known by his girl as he really was, or *thought* he was.

Healthy young people are touched only casually by those whose products abuse the new freedom which surrounds sex. And the censorship of such material does not remove the fantasies of needful, not-so-healthy young people who focus on sex to gain acceptance and a self-image they feel they can live with.

Perhaps then the most important aim is, within this new freedom, to develop positive and healthy attitudes toward the self. It will be just this that allows for the construction of practical standards which will in turn issue in deeper and more meaningful relationships, premarital and postmarital, among the younger people of this time of transition.

The Janices, the Erics and Marges, the Bruces, Carolyns and Berts, and all of their peers know what they don't want, and they have an idea about where to go constructively from here. They do not, most of them, covet the role of libertine, for they instinctively avoid the chaos and license that role produces. But they cannot, on the other hand, accept the old; it is gone, but all gone.

Where do they go from here? What can be said that makes useful sense? What are the issues they see themselves facing? What are the questions young people are asking, and *how* do they ask them?

It is time to listen to them and learn.

ISSUES THAT ACHE

The Pressures

Young people do not treat their concerns casually. They see them as issues that ache. And one of their painful concerns is that of preserving identity amid the pressures that would obscure that identity. They are aware of the tendency to treat persons as if they were things. The late Martin Buber measured sensitively this trend, which comes oddly enough within the currents that would emancipate man from racial or political or personal or male-female restrictions. Buber feels that the person is treated as if he were already on the mortician's slab. Man is approached as primarily biological or psychological or political or socio-logical or organizational—as a thing.

Or, in any other form, man is served up *en masse*. He is valued as a service*man*, country*man*, clergy*man*, sales*man;* as one unit in a mass category, as a thing.

And this raises a two-sided question: How can I be a true person, an honest-to-God human being, and, how can I as a person enter into significant relationships with other persons? Again in Buber's terminology: I want to be an "I" and not an "it" and I want to relate myself to a "thou" and not to an "it" (to another person and not to a thing). How can I be myself, and be in relationship with other real people?

The Self

So acutely in this century, and especially in this culture, men and women, old as well as young, are searching for a sense of self, a sense that they are somebodies who matter. And they want an adequate degree of security for the self they discover. Frequently, however, it cannot be found. The self shivers in its loneliness. The self stutters in its attempt to communicate. The self stampedes in its effort to be of significant value personally. The self stands in the silence of its failure and inadequacies.

The self: we have been trained in our culture to sublimate the self, to keep it down and passive, to enforce a heavy-handed control over its assertiveness. And in doing so, we have deeply scarred the self, and reimprisoned it at the very moment it had an opportunity for release and freedom never known before. We have so eclipsed the self, the person, that we lose ourselves, lose our identities, even our souls.

What then are the live concerns indicated by this aching question of the self? They are many, and they are important, for out of the depths of each individual come these questions basic to man's nature. To be human is to ask them and to look for real answers.

(I) *Who am I?* The basis for this question is the search of the self for *identity,* or in a good clinical term, self-definition. What makes up the "real me" and does it matter that I am at all? Am I unique, or merely an accidental combination of protoplasm and genes? How much of a solitary individual am I truly? *Who am I?*

(II) *Wherefore am I?* The second basic human concern is the search of the self for *purpose.* Is there a reason for my existence as a self? Is there a goal or purpose my particular life is to attain? Where am I going and is it purposeful? *Wherefore am I?*

(III) *Why am I?* And with these two questions, a third arises, concerned with the search of the self for *meaning*. Do I as a self have value? Is there essential and abiding meaning to the person I am? Does it really matter whether I exist or do not exist? *Why am I?*

Identity. Purpose. Meaning. These three are the pivots around which life—the self—gathers in its significance. And these are not minor matters, for we need as humans to be deeply assured that we do in fact have personal value and significance. We need to define and understand the identity, purpose and meaning which make us unique, for without such definition, the self degenerates into a nervous and insecure blur. With such definition, we can with certainty claim our identities as selves, as well as the meaning and purpose of those selves.

Claiming Our Identity

To claim our identity is the measure of maturity: the desire and capacity to "take over" our lives and be and do something that, while not necessarily spectacular, is of consequence. To disown the search for identity is to lose, by choice or by default, our essential humanity, our personal uniqueness.

The self is to be asserted, not neglected. The pressures of the times, however, conspire to make us neglectful, causing the young even greater confusion. They are told from parent to pulpit not to be selfish, not to use or abuse other people. Selfishness is the cardinal sin. And such teachings are essentially right, but this is where a sad confusion comes in. For so often the injunction to not be selfish is misinterpreted to be an order or command to be self-*less*. This is a serious misunderstanding, which requires further and important scrutiny.

To be unselfish is not to be self-less, for this is to be no self at all. Rather we are to be self-*full,* that is, full of the self we are, having a maximum of personal identity and unfolding that identity in a purposeful and meaningful and active life. The person with a strong sense of self is in much better shape potentially to combat and overthrow his innate selfishness. Selfishness is a cancer to the fully developed self. Obviously it makes sense that selfishness is our mortal enemy, and, as a matter of fact, would be all too glad to betray the self into self-lessness. For a self-less person lacks self-definition and integrity. A self-less person is simply a nobody. This common error of saying that we are to be self-less in order not to be selfish only leads us away from the questions which we, by nature, must ask: Who am I? Wherefore am I? Why am I?

Actually, the self is the only thing we really have. We may have possessions, but they are a means of communicating ourselves to others. We may have good brains or develop extraordinary skills, but these too are a means of expressing the self in work or school or home. If a guy gives his girl a bouquet of flowers or a box of candy or his fraternity pin, these are but symbols of the affection he has for her. Finally, the only thing he truly has to give to her is the person—the self—that he is. And it is likewise true that this unique person is what she cares about and wants. The self, once again, is all that we possess and have to give. To drain ourselves of it would be to make sex, along with everything else, empty and meaningless. Therefore, it is not too much to say that to abandon the self is to abandon life.

Subverting the Self

And yet our kind of society appears to be conspiring to undermine the self, to obscure and subvert it. Forces from all corners of contemporary life seem engaged in aggressively depersonalizing man, and this affects his attitude toward his sexual conduct just as it does other areas of his life. We are in an advanced technological age, and yet we are told that this is only the hors d'oeuvre stage of technological development; the main course is yet to come.

One of the results already apparent is that a man is increasingly measured by the function he can perform, not by the person he is. He qualifies for a life's work because of the job description he can fill. Man, the self, along with his work and his sex and his life generally becomes functionalized. The work becomes more important than the worker. The image becomes more important than the person. The sex act becomes more important than what is meant by and through it. This functionalization of personality pervades all of contemporary life.

As one recent college graduate now engaged in the business world wrote:

> The fellows up in personnel
> They have a set of cards on me.
> The sprinkled perforations tell
> My individuality.
>
> And what am I? I am a chart
> On the cards of IBM.
> The secret places of my heart
> Have little secrecy to them.
>
> It matters not how much I prate,
> How charged with punishment the scroll,
> The files are masters of my fate,
> Those perforations are the captains of my soul.
>
> On Sunday night my brain began to buzz,
> I was in agony all the night.
> On Monday I found out what the trouble was:
> Personnel had my paperclip on too tight!

Self-Love?

If all that we have been saying is true, that we are to be self-full rather than self-less, what are the implications for the love of one's self? Again, this has a suspicious sound; it doesn't seem quite proper to be overly concerned with how we love ourselves. Nevertheless it is a decisive concern which needs further probing, and which has direct consequences upon our entire approach to sexual conduct.

We operate on several levels of love relationship: the self to itself, the self to others, the self to nature and the self to God. But self-love stands at the center of all of these relationships. And this is not contrary, as has been often inferred, to biblical Christianity. "Thou shalt love thy neighbor *as* thyself." This is the second great commandment given by Christ. That is to say, you are to love others in the same manner in which you love yourself. This is strictly true. For we extend to others the kind of love which we have for ourselves. If our self-love is healthy, then the love we extend to others is in turn healthy. But if our self-love is unhealthy and distorted—that is, if we don't like or care about ourselves very much, or at all—then the love we extend toward others is likewise diseased and distorted. In short, we cannot love someone else with a love different from the love we bear to ourselves. We cannot give a love that we do not have for ourselves; all we have is the *kind of love* with which we love and accept ourselves.

Therefore, it matters terribly what kind of love, acceptance, care, we have for our own persons, body and mind. Christ also says that a sick fig tree cannot bear good fruit, only bad. A sick person's love is, in the same manner, sick love. How essential it is then that we have a strong and healthy self-love. The quality of all other relationships depends upon this.

Other Loves

This self-love, and the manner of it, is not however isolated and insulated from other people and from life generally. It is from the springs of self-love that we enter into a love relationship with others, with nature and with God. We want to love and respect and accept ourselves. But quite as much do we need to be loved and respected and accepted by others. To be human, we need to draw others into our own personal love orbit. Man is built to be a lover!

All this is for our own well-being. And it is not confined just to other human beings. We extend our feelings, our love, toward the worlds of animal and natural life as well: a beautiful scene, an exquisite flower, a favorite dog.

And, finally, we search for God, to be loved by Him and to love Him to the fullest possible extent. To seek, to know and to love God—this too is built into the human creature. Man instinctively wonders about God: who He is, what He is like, what He cares about, how He operates and why. Is God a lover, too? And what kind of love is His? We shall see later what His love means positively in regard to faith, love and sex.

Self-Alienation

Self-love is not an easy art. For the life of the self is not neatly packaged and unproblematic. In experience we often find the self in a state of being alienated or estranged from itself. Much is being said about estrangement; our literature is full of it: the many situations of marital alienation, the so-called dislocation of the psyche, the alienation of people and races, the severe distortion and elimination of the human shape or figure in much of modern art. It is not just a matter of turning on the spigot of self-love until our well-being overfloweth, for in the midst of life we know and experience tension, separation, alienation, on all levels of relationship.

The person who is alienated from himself is the unhappiest of creatures. And this can take many forms, the most common being self-rejection. To reject one's self, whatever form it takes—intellectual, emotional, physical, sexual—causes great and painful tensions and can produce severe unbalance or mental and emotional dislocation.

Alienation makes a person uncertain and insecure about his own essential self. It can take the form of self-depreciation, fear of failure or inadequacy, fear of rejection by others in the present or future. To wonder if you can accept your own body, physically and sexually, is not at all an unusual problem for young people. They do wonder and they do need to know if who they are and if what they have, physically and sexually, is good enough; and often they are hard on themselves in their self-appraisal.

And if one is unsure of himself, and bewildered about his own value as a person, this can cause him to separate himself from others, or at least from any deep relationship with others. He may want to hide from others rather than reveal himself, and so he, like Bruce, may take on a certain kind of "personality role." He fears that if his contemporaries really knew him as he is or as he thinks he is, they would promptly reject him even as he has rejected himself. Rather than engage boldly in life, he prefers to stay partially disengaged, and save the hurt of the rejection he thinks he really deserves. Of course, these feelings can be minor and mild in some, but in others they are strong and dominant. Whatever the degree, a person who is alienated from himself is not only aching within, he is also separated from other people, and often very lonely in his self-despair. As one college student, who can communicate only to an indifferent piece of paper, writes:

> Retreat from nothing
> To nothing find;
> Who attacks?
> Who lurks behind
> My imaginings?
> Bearer of darkness—
> In chilled fear, Why
> Cover thou me
> In thy black shrouds?
> My lonely soul lurches
> From my solitary—
> Cruel joke, cutting jab—
> How can I live with thee
> My solitude?
> Lonely love,
> Lecherous lure,
> Limp life,
> Retreats from nothing
> To nothing find.

The alienated self tends to fly apart. The self when too greatly estranged from itself is sick.

But, as with self-love, self-alienation spreads not only into one's relationships (or lack of significant relationships) with others, but with nature and God as well. When one is out of tune with himself, he tends to take this out on the natural world too. He may enjoy beating his dog, or plundering the neighbor's beautiful garden or smashing street lights. He can be exploitative not only of other people to meet his unhealthy needs, but of animals or property as well.

And this self-alienated man or woman is going to be estranged from and angry at God, the God who could not conceivably love such an undesirable, and the God who likely caused the despicable situation in the first place. Therefore, he tends to give God hostility rather than love, and his confusion enlarges. He is caught, as we all are, in the confusion of wanting to love and be loved—for he indeed, as we have said, is built to be a lover—and feeling that he can neither love himself nor be loved by man or God. This can be an intense and incapacitating fear or merely a tempered unsettling, but it lurks with all, as one of the essential human characteristics.

A man or woman grows or does not grow by the way he handles this tension between self-love and self-estrangement. And as we have intimated earlier, growing is an art, not a skill. It does not come automatically but haltingly and with struggle. It is, like it or not, the way of life.

Love's Growingness

We need to expand further on how love grows to see this issue in its fullest dimension. Love is not a personality trait. It can enlarge, or be blocked at some indiscriminate point, or it can wither and die. Love is a *developed capacity* of human beings.

We are born with the capacity to love but little more. As babies, this capacity must be awakened and stimulated, and as we are loved by our parents, we respond with love. From the experiences of being loved, we begin to fill in our capacity to love in response like fitting in the pieces of a jugsaw puzzle.

How greatly it matters then what kind of love we received from our parents, and what kind of love we will as parents give our own children. If the parental love we received was substantially unhealthy, our own capacity to give and receive love will be scarred, perhaps even incapacitated. Sorokin describes those who are seriously deformed emotionally by a sick parental love as having a "trained incapacity" to receive love, much less give it.

And indeed experience indicates that sometimes it is much harder to be the receiver of love than the giver. To accept love puts certain demands upon the receiver. To accept the love of another is also to accept the responsibility for handling that love. This is why love must develop cautiously. For to enlarge the capacity to love experientially is to trust increasingly that the love we extend will not be manhandled by the receiver. To give love is to make one's self open and vulnerable and subject to hurt. Therefore we do not casually give our love completely on sight, but gradually, to the degree that we trust it will be well cared for; and we receive more and more to the degree we can feel responsible for the gift of love given.

And so we are born into a world populated essentially by one person, mother. We learn what it is to receive and give love from our experience of that world. Gradually we learn to trust the love of others in ever larger circles. We develop friends, best friends and confidants. Then as we hit the later teens we focus on the few with whom we feel freest to be ourselves. We have developed, hopefully, the capacity for deep love and secure trust. And then we tend to spell this out in terms of that one person with whom we can be the most open and intimate—the person we want to marry.

By then we have come full circle. But love does not stop growing upon selection of a mate! It is more like beginning again. Within courtship and engagement the love relationship *must* grow and become more and more secure even as the persons become more and more vulnerable. And even more than that, love *must* continue to grow after marriage, especially perhaps after the honeymoon. In fact, the growth of love knows no limit. Love can be likened to a many-faceted diamond. Not all facets are illuminated at one time, and part of its grandeur is that it sparkles in an infinite number of ways, always in a new and changing constellation of lights and colors.

Love is developmental, the enlarging capacity to trust and to be open to give willingly and receive tenderly. Love that does not grow stalls and bankrupts. Even at best, love does not grow evenly; it is hammered out in experience, possibly through painful situations, often through the processes of alienation and restoration. And this restoration comes through love's special capacity to give and receive forgiveness. Love the developed art, requiring at times much endeavor, is the same love which is a many-splendored thing!

CHRISTIANITY MISREPRESENTED

3

There is nothing like a cluttered up Christianity to add to the normal confusion relating to sexual mores and practices, and certainly the front *and* the back yards of Christianity are littered with much debris. All kinds of practices and prohibitions concerning human sexuality are alleged in the name of Christianity, and our first concern must be to clear away, once and for all, this clutter. Only then can we begin to see and appreciate what an authentic Christian attitude toward sex is. And we may be in for some good, and wanted, surprises.

Anti-Material Spirituality

One of the most common misrepresentations of the Christian position is that its spirituality is anti-material. This view holds, supposedly in the name of Christ, that the material is inferior to the spiritual. Although the physical is man's plight, and is necessary to continue the human species, the physical-sexual is more to be endured than enjoyed. Sex can be justified on the grounds of procreation, but one must be extremely cautious not to become enslaved to the lust and power of the flesh. According to this misrepresentation of Christianity the body must be kept down!

The body is dangerously distracting to the spiritual dimension of life, and the latter is man's true good and the purpose of his life. The flesh can all too easily be the cause of the spirit's downfall: in fact, this is precisely the intention of the flesh, to subvert man from his higher nature. So the argument goes; all supposedly dictated by Christianity.

Moral Negativity

Another point of view robed in the garb of Christianity comes from that inevitable group of people who would like to structure tightly every moment of a person's existence with rules and regulations. They, too, think that Christianity considers the physical and the sexual essentially nasty, even after marriage. Their highly detailed formulas for what one can do, must do and cannot do are for the most part negative in intent. They cite that Christ never once mentioned sex and that Paul was, at least at one point, pointedly negative about it. In any event, they assume that sexual practices must be guarded by an elaborate series of "do not's," threatening consequences which range all the way from an eternity in hell to punishment by contracting some dread disease.

Such a view runs counter to the real intent of morality, as we shall shortly see; but the fact remains that many hold it to be strictly Christian.

Young people rebel, and rightly so, from such a negative and constrictive viewpoint. If this is Christianity, they say, then market it someplace else to someone else. If this is Christianity it is plainly not allowing for natural sexual desire and expression. And they conclude that Christianity is dead set against their having any fun, that it frowns heavily on any pleasure in sexual relations, absolutely so before marriage. Some even conclude that Christianity is irrelevantly moralistic in forbidding premarital expression, which they feel could well prepare them for the sexual skills that are a definite aid to sex within marriage.

Neither of these views—an anti-material spirituality and a moral negativeness—nor any subsidiary to them and customarily ascribed to Christianity are in fact authentically Christian.

Will the Real Christianity Please Stand Up?

The time has come to clear away some of this debris and discern the mainstream of Christian thought regarding the material and the moral. We may be in for some surprises. What, truly, is the Christian attitude about the material, about the physical and the sexual? What is the Christian position toward the purpose and function of morals and of morality generally?

God Made It!

A serious survey of the Bible shows irrefutably that Christianity is pro-material. God made the material. God saw that it was good. He loved what He had made. God did not simply create man's soul and then imprison it in a physical body which could only inflict grievous problems upon the soul. Such a God would be cantankerous, if not actually malicious! And if God loves what He creates, which He deems good, ought we not take the same posture toward not only the material, but the physical and sexual as well? God did not say that this certain part of His creation is good (man's soul) and this other part is bad (man's body). He looked at His whole creation, and He said that *all of it* was good and the object of His love.

Therefore, the material is to be treated in a first-class, rather than second-class, manner—seriously, for its own sake. As we have said before, and would reinforce, the physical-sexual is essentially man's friend, not his enemy, though assuredly man can *use* his materiality in a way damaging to himself and others. The key word is *use*. Sex does not use the man; he has considerable and significant control over his sexuality. Man uses sex; and the kind of use determines the consequences good or bad. But in the beginning it was made by God, and He saw it as good, and to be used by us for good.

Christ Redeemed It!

But having said that all of God's world, including the material, was created by Him and pronounced good is only to begin. There is an even more decisive point in any Christian discussion of the material and physical. And that point is the person of Christ. The Christian faith maintains that God in the person of Christ is the full self-disclosure of God in time and space, in materiality. We call this event the Incarnation: God's full involvement of Himself in the created world, and not in just certain aspects (like the mind or soul), but in every aspect, including the physical. The coming of God in Christ was, in short, psychophysical, that is, full and complete: mind, soul and *body*. "And the Word was made flesh, and dwelt among us, (and we beheld his glory, the glory as of the only begotten of the Father,) full of grace and truth" (John 1:14, K.J.V.).

The church specifically rejected all ideas that God's involvement in Christ was either partial or part-time. God in Christ "infleshed" Himself wholly into the human situation. He lived man's life and died man's death. His involvement in the order and nature of the created world was comprehensive and complete. And the church has never been willing to compromise in any manner this position, for the importance and relevance of Christianity pivots on this basic premise.

The Incarnation therefore has immediate and direct

implications concerning God's continuing care for the
material. It is to say, first of all, that Christ is pro-material.
He considers the material and physical not only a proper
but also a worthy way of direct access to His world. If God
so considers the material, in both creating and redeeming
it (making it whole and wholesome once again), how could
Christianity conceivably take up a negative and unwhole-
some view? The main thrust of Christianity is "down" into
the whole of the created order, not "up" and away from it.
This is what the Incarnation means, and why the late and
gifted Archbishop of Canterbury, William Temple, would
say that Christianity is by far the most materialistic of the
major religions.

Secondly, the incarnational point of view is most
compatible with the judgment of both medicine and psy-
chiatry that man is not a collection of basic attributes: one
part spiritual, one part mental, one part emotional, one
part willful and a last part physical; and that these parts,
or chunks, more or less coexist within human beings.
Rather the modern physician would contend that these
capacities are locked irrevocably together in man; they
can be separated only in analysis, not in experience.

When a person is less than whole and divided into
parts, there is damage to his personality and how it func-
tions. Cannon Douglas Rhymes in his book *No New Morality*
points out:

> It is when we see ourselves as a whole—a whole
> which is to be loved for its wholeness, not divided
> into higher and lower—that we begin to love our-
> selves, to love the flesh, the mind and the spirit, be-
> cause the flesh, the mind and the spirit are me, and
> the more I know about myself, the more I respect my-
> self. The less I feel guilty in myself, the more I

shall respect, know and love others. . . . the only
guilt I need feel is when I have ceased to be myself and . . . am pretending to be what I am not, and
calling it good.[1]

In short, man is a psychophysical creature, an irreducible unity of body, mind and spirit. It is that whole
creature, all of him, that God creates and loves, to the
extent that He places Himself fully with the human situation.
Thereby in Christ God places the highest value on the
material and the physical, while leaving us free to *use*,
mis*use*, or ab*use* these gifts.

Morality: For Our Well-Being

Certainly Christianity has a morality, a view of right
ideals and principles of human conduct; but, as we have
seen, the Christian morality is often misunderstood and
misconstrued. Any belief in any god has implications for
the structure and discipline of the believer's life. A religion
without an ensuing morality is only half a religion, for if
it does not affect one's life, of what consequence is it? If
we are not concerned to *do* what we *believe*, then our religion is of the "cold slops" variety.

This is not to say that morals and morality should be
negative and prohibitive in their intent. In any event,
this is not true of Christianity, though Christianity has
been used, yea exploited, to such ends as we have illustrated.
At this point we must ask what is the *source* and the *intention*
of morality, for it is not a thing in itself. Moral codes do not
emerge from a vacuum, but are the codal implications
drawn from what we believe about God and man. What we
specifically believe about God's purpose for man gives

[1] Douglas Rhymes, *No New Morality* (New York: The Bobbs-Merrill
Company, Inc., 1964), pp. 29 f.

concrete shape to our behavior man to man, and thereby produces a moral code. Thus, morals are dependent upon and derivative from belief, from theology. What we believe should determine what we do, and not the other way around. Too often however morals become divorced from belief or, worse, dominate it. It can become entirely possible to have a set of morals that have no real relationship with what is believed. Those who say that Christian morality is properly negative and prohibitive, for example, are taking their own moral notions and simply trying to give them authority and credence by calling them Christian. This is intolerable to the informed Christian.

Correctly understood, what we believe about God and his world and about man contours the view we have about right ideals and principles of human conduct. In short, theology shapes morality. Whatever guides for human conduct we have then should flow directly from our Christian estimate of God and from God's purpose for His world and all His creatures. And precisely because we have seen God's intention and purpose for man to be positive, we must see that any Christian guidelines to human behavior or morality are likewise positive. Christian morality, then, is positive, not negative; liberating, not confining or restricting. It can open the way to the deepest, most significant kinds of relationships between persons, and between God and His people.

Morality is for our well-being. It is essentially for us, not against us. There are proper and positive safeguards to protect sexual expression from misuse. For our own well-being, and for the well-being of others, "Thou shalt not . . ." For to do so is only to inflict damage upon our own persons, as well as others. Such a view of Christian morality is then indeed positive in its intention. It would protect us from any kind of action, sexual and otherwise, which would defeat the deep meaning and purpose of personal love. A Christian morality exists to help us be the "honest-to-God persons" we were created to be. It unclutters the way for the deepest person-to-person communication which human beings potentially, not automatically, are meant to have.

Christian morality is then the manner in which we discipline and structure our lives so that we do not abuse ourselves or one another, and so that we are more open to the deepest and most meaningful kinds of personal relationships. Such Christian discipline is constructive. Discipline in this light is no longer something getting in the way of life, and of our fun! Discipline is a way of opening up dimensions of life where we can become "honest-to-God persons."

Thus we can say that the true *source* of morality is theology; it is the belief in God and His purpose. The true *intention* of morality is human well-being; it is the deep and significant personal interplay between people and groups of people. Christian morality is for man, not against him.

LOVE
MISUNDERSTOOD

4

Having dealt with some of the unfortunate misunderstandings of the Christian view of the material and physical, we must now do the same for the subject of love. For here too expectations are often distorted and exaggerated and subsequently become major sources of disillusionment. Carolyn had impassioned hopes for the sexual act only to find her hopes about the climax shattered. Cliff's advice to his heated fraternity brother was that in his experience sex was not all it was cracked up to be: "If that's all sex is, there's really not so much to it after all." Such misunderstandings can cause bitterness, or boredom, or disillusionment or personality disfigurement.

Love Is Not . . .

Love is not the Sunday newspaper supplement's questionnaire: "Do you love your husband? Take the test below and see!"

Love is not to be found in the perfume ad which promises the user the inevitable.

Love is not the shadowy look that flashes across the faces of a Richard Burton and an Elizabeth Taylor as the sun quietly drops to leave them alone in the privacy of the night.

Love is not simply in the specifications of "body-boy brawn" or the shapely contours of a 36-24-36 figure.

Love is not the IBM-like coordination of two differing or similar sets of family background.

Love is not the status attained, or attainable, by being seen with, or married to, someone who is "with it."

Love is not an open invitation to be used, or seduced or raped.

Love is not the capacity to have intercourse.

Love is not a surface matter, at least for human beings. For unlike other creatures of the animal world, the human has considerable control over his sexual urges and actions. Sex comes seasonally for the higher animals, and they "do what comes naturally." This is however not an option for the human of the species.

Men and women are lovers, not sexers. Our love centers in personality, in the very heart of our persons. For us it cannot be simply when a "body meets a body," for this is to depersonalize our capacities to give and receive love, to give and receive deeply of one another's whole person. In other words, conscious love marks us off from other creatures, and we consciously express that love through our thoughts, words and actions.

The capacity of love is at the center of our personalities and is as complex as our personalities themselves. We are fooled when we think love is something simple we do with someone; there would be very little, or at least too little, personal encounter if love were merely a certain kind of activity. Love viewed in such a manner is cheapened and diluted love, and it cannot last long. The gift of the capacity to love and be loved is no small gift! To put it as clearly and succinctly as possible:

Love can be just as dangerous as it is delightful.
Love can be just as divisive as it is unitive.
Love can be just as possessive as it is liberating.
Love can be just as boring as it is fulfilling.

If we exchange the word "sex" for the word "love" in the above assertions, we have a second set of truths.

Love is delightful when there is a free and uninhibited flow of openness, of trust and respect, of mutually desired action. Love is dangerous when it lays open the whole realm of inner and private feelings and thoughts to be handled, and perhaps hurt, by the other person.

Love is unitive when a couple develops a deep sense of oneness in their ideas, and emotions and their bodies. Love is divisive when thoughtlessness or selfishness turns the relationship, even if for a moment, into an occasion for mental, emotional or sexual exploitation of the other person.

Love is liberating when within the intimacy of relationship it frees individuals to be themselves even at their respective worst. Love is possessive when it tends to suck a person into an exclusive, well-protected, solitary relationship.

Love is fulfilling when the relationship is entered into unreservedly and generously, with a genuine sensitivity to the needs of self and those of the other person. Love is boring when it becomes a routine activity of dates, or conversation or even of sexual intercourse. Once again, if we substitute the word "sex" for the word "love" in the above we see a deeper meaning to the relationship of love and sex.

Disturbances in Love and Sex

Such are some of the tensions surrounding love and sex, and they are intensified in everyday experience. We

live in a culture that excessively overlays sexual experience with a romantic pall, and this complicates the situation for many. Thoughts and emotions and sexuality are real
things, and are to be treated in a realistic manner. By realism here we do not mean that we are to treat our experience
in some kind of dull and negligent manner. Nor do we mean
that we are to strip all the romantic aspects from love and
sex, but only those that give us a goal unattainable in actual
experience. There is little point to try to live for something
that cannot be. This is not to take the joy and pleasure
out of love and sex but to have the genuine joy and pleasure
which experience itself holds out to us. A realistic rather
than overly-romantic approach to love and sex and their
interrelationship will make it a lot easier to be on the right
track.

The Two Sexes

There are natural tensions in any relationship, as Eric
and Marge already know, and these will always be. Life
would be dull indeed if there were not a categorical difference between a man and a woman beyond the simply
physical. For the male person is also built mentally and
emotionally in a way that is different from the female. The
differentiation between the two sexes involves far more
than a difference in sexual apparatus. And thank God for
that! Because the two sexes are structured psychophysi-
cally* in distinct ways, we have infinite possibilities of
kinds of relationship between them. No relationship therefore need become deadly and dull, for the male brings to it
something distinctively male as the female brings what
singularly she is. If people understood that members of the
opposite sex were of a significantly different cut, many of

---

* (I.e., an irreducible oneness of body and mind.)

their tensions would be unnecessary, and, more than that, they could more fully enjoy the difference!

This differentiation between the two sexes, like love and sex, is shaped by how it is used or employed. This natural tension between them can become unnatural, and can become the unhappy basis for a lack of understanding. The tendencies to misjudge or misinterpret the other person become the grounds for antagonism, which when accumulated produce hostility. Resentment may spring up when what was expected from the other person is not forthcoming according to the specifications laid down consciously or unconsciously in advance.

A real momentum of rising hostility and rejection gathers in such uneasy relationships. No one is infallible in judging another person, even one intimately close; but intimacy is a tender relationship and can go flying off base with unusual ease. We might define this tendency as a tension between our own special set of needs and those of the other person, and we gravitate toward giving our needs the priority! We can use a small but packed word to describe this: *sin*—the inclination to elevate ourselves to a higher degree of importance by depressing or neglecting the other person. Sin is the shorthand word for that drive toward egomania in us all, an unrelenting drive stronger than the sex drive itself.

Ambivalent?

Another form of this same tension is our ambivalence about love. On the one hand, we desire deep in our bones to love, to give ourselves wholeheartedly to someone we care greatly about. On the other hand and with at least equal force, we want to be loved. To love—to be loved: one strains to be dominant over the other. When "to love" is the dominating need, a person is saying "I'm the big lover!" so as to prove himself strong and sure when he is not. When "to be loved" is dominant, he is saying, "Here, take me; give me all I need," so as to have all his needs enfolded by the other person. In either dominance, the ego requirements of the one are insensitive to, if not ignoring, not only the needs of the other but his own as well. What was a natural tension has issued into an egocentric, selfish, sinful predicament.

Such tensions are not only the property of the married. They enter into any male-female relationship, and the more the young couple is alert to their own natures and to their (psychophysical) differences, the greater the chances that they will not be seduced mentally, emotionally or sexually by each other or by sin. This is all part of the realism with which Christianity approaches the normalities and abnormalities which are a part of every relationship.

Your Expectations

Another area, closely related to that of an open-eyed realism concerning the relationship between the sexes, concerns what two people *expect* of each other. It is natural enough to want the one we love to be the greatest person in the world, to be near-perfect, godlike. But with too much idealism and too little realism, we can impose expectations upon the person, or the love act (as with Carolyn) or upon ourselves to the extent that we become embittered when they fail.

No one can be a junior deity for another person. Christians should know that they do not have to play the game of God. They are already aware of the God in whom they believe, and that He is their God, for *both* of them. Therefore, they need not have unreasonable and troublesome expectations of each other. This is not, of course, permission to be the lowest form of human being, but it does take the edge off the frequent demands we place on each other to be someone we cannot possibly be.

If we do not have to be divine to each other, we *can* be free to be human! And, by the way, that is precisely what God wants us to be: fully, authentically human. We are to expect neither too much *nor* too little. This is not always easy to do, for we do want the best. But when we want or demand too much, consciously or unconsciously, we are in the grip of a different form of sin. "I will be your God—worship me!"—or—"You must be God to me, or else I will give my 'worship' up!" To abstain from forcing someone into a characterization that he is not, and to be able to take each other as each person is: these are essential forms of Christian realism.

What? Forgive Him!

Toward the end of chapter 2 we discussed the many kinds of alienation that can crop up between two people developing a relationship. We alluded briefly to love's capacity for reconciliation through forgiveness. In the light of our immediate discussion, forgiveness now comes into full focus.

Oddly enough and with interesting implications, for many in this day forgiveness is a sign of weakness, of undignifiedly giving in when the other person deserves only rejection and scorn. In this all-too-common view forgiveness is seen as no more than capitulating to the offender and letting him get away with his abuse.

Forgiveness, however, is a form of strength rather than of weakness. It is much more difficut than executing some suitable revenge. Therefore, in any developing relationship between two people there needs to be genuine understanding of the dynamics of forgiveness, particularly as forgiveness is one of the most important ways that love spells itself out in action. Love-in-action, by means of forgiveness, is therapeutic to alienated relationships; it is an action of healing and reconciliation. Without it, an alienated relationship can only continue in separation and hostility. No relationship can endure, let alone grow, unless the capacity for forgiveness is present and active.

Nor is it too much to say that forgiveness is a highly complicated capacity if it is authentic. Actually, we need to have insight into *three* levels of forgiveness if we are to appreciate the fullness of this uniquely human capacity. They are the capacities: (I) to forgive, (II) to be forgiven and (III) to forgive oneself.

(I) The capacity to forgive. When we have been hurt gravely by someone, our first impulse certainly is not to forgive that person. It is to get back at him, taking a suitable revenge for the harm to person or pride we have received. In the first flush, we want to return the abuse in kind, perhaps even with additional abusiveness. If the offender is someone we care about, our feelings are stronger and our reactions more complicated and confused. Since we are more tender or "hurt prone" with those we love, we react to their offense in a jumble of anger, embarrassment, disappointment and a desire to return punishment. Only our love and compassion can check us, but this increases our confusion as to what we should feel and do.

The painfulness of being hurt through abuse or falsehood or misrepresentation or neglect thunders in our consciousness. However severely they may have been hurt, few are willing to break off, once and for all, a relationship which had been characterized by love or friendship. The relationship might be shattered, but even as we nurse our wounds, most of us would not want it lost altogether. On the other hand, the sinful act has been done and it cannot be undone. It has become an indelible part of the "history" of that particular relationship. But can it be overcome and healed? However much we may desire the restoration of a once important relationship, we cannot have it back by trying to forget or minimize the offense. The offense must be confronted by both the offended and the offender and together they must overcome it consciously and openly. They must find the means of expressing their love in such a way that forgiveness becomes operational between them. Love must express itself between them as the sincere request for, and the genuine giving of, forgiveness. The first level of forgiveness, to forgive, is hard work.

(II) The capacity to be forgiven. It is very difficult to give genuine forgiveness to someone even when we want to. But it is even more difficult for the one who has caused the offense to receive the forgiveness of the offended person. The problem of receiving forgiveness becomes all too apparent when we, in the face of our wretchedness toward another, are returned a love so deep as to forgive. The action of authentic forgiveness reveals clearly enough to the offender how great a contrast there is between his sin and the other person's love. And when we have been the offender and know that we are in fact forgiven, it is entirely possible for us to feel even more badly about what we have done. We may resent the other's capacity to forgive us in the face of our misuse or abuse of them. We may sense a deep and uncomfortable judgment along with the forgiveness. It is then far from easy to be able to receive forgiveness. In fact, the deeper the forgiveness offered, the more difficult it is to receive. Therefore the second level of any "transaction" of forgiveness, to receive it, is perhaps a more difficult task than to forgive. Only a steady and mature love can make it work.

(III) The capacity to forgive oneself. There is yet a third aspect to the dynamics of forgiveness if it is to be completely satisfactory, and restore a broken relationship. It is much neglected but altogether essential. Having been forgiven, it is equally important to go on to forgive oneself. Though we may be quite sure of the forgiveness we have received, unless we then proceed to forgive ourselves, the action is not completed. In that case the fullness of the forgiveness, and of the reconciliation, has not become completely operative, the relationship not truly restored. It is, at best, "scotch-taped" together. Only when the forgiveness is truly taken in, and healing infiltrates and enables self-forgiveness, can it be said that the dynamic of forgiveness has gone full-route. Again, only self-love has the ability to produce self-forgiveness.

The action then of any true forgiveness is complex, not simple. It is mindful, not forgetful; difficult, not easy; continual hard work, not simply automatic. To forgive, to receive forgiveness and to forgive ourselves are not only on the deepest levels of our need, they are also some of the most difficult demands that can be placed upon us. They require love, which, acting as forgiveness, alone can make a splintered relationship whole once again. Love is asked for precisely at a point when to love is the most difficult thing in the world to do; to love the unlovable, to forgive the unforgivable. A forgiveness not motivated and empowered by love cannot deal with the alienation and hostilities that can separate a man and woman. Without love as the source of forgiveness, an alienated relationship enlarges and festers until it comes at last to a painful and tortured "death." For any young couple in love and considering marriage, an essential measure of the growing maturity of their relationship is their ability to operate in depth on all three levels of forgiveness. They will need these capacities and if their developing love is strong and steady then they will have them.

Christianity correctly represented. Love deeply understood and lived. Forgiveness profoundly operative. These three factors form the bedrock of any penetrating insight into faith, sex and love.

A "HIGH" VIEW OF
LOVE AND SEX

5

We are affirming that intrinsic to an authentic under-standing of Christianity is a high viewpoint of love and sex. We are saying that because a person controls his sexuality, rather than being controlled by it, he can use or misuse it. In other words, sex is not sin, but sin can use sex in such a way as to distort and exploit person-to-person relationships. Christianity calls us to significant and satisfying use of sexuality. We are not called away from sex but from sin; and we are summoned to depth relationships. The sexual aspect is one central means of expressing deep relationship.

Let Liturgy Say It

We have observed that past moral codes held by some denominations of Christianity have had a low view of sex, and probably of love as well; but that these groups were not in the mainstream of Christianity. Perhaps we can see this in another light by inspecting the "preface" to a service of holy matrimony. Liturgy is the way in which we worship, and in this case celebrate a marriage. Liturgy tells us quite as much as do theology or morality. Indeed liturgy, and here a marriage liturgy, is our way of acting out together what we believe, what our theology actually is in action. We go to an old and revered and traditional marriage liturgy in the Book of Common Prayer to see what estimate is placed upon the relationship between a man and a woman.

The "preface" in part reads:

> Dearly beloved, we are gathered together here in the sight of God, and in the face of this company, to join together this Man and this Woman in holy Matrimony; which is an honorable estate, instituted of God, signifying unto us the mystical union that is betwixt Christ and His Church: . . . and therefore is not by any to be entered into unadvisedly or lightly; but reverently, discreetly, advisedly, soberly, and in the fear [awe] of God.

A Private Affair?

Three main things are said here which deserve our thoughtful concern. First, that the relationship between a man and a woman, before or after marriage, is not simply a private one—"and in the face of this company." Any relationship between human beings involves a lot more than just the two of them, and they cannot, if they are responsible, tell the rest of the world to go rot. They came from a social setting, and indeed if their relationship is a sound and good one their love for each other will overflow into other relationships. Before or after marriage, their relationship does not exist in a vacuum but in a whole constellation of interaction and responsibilities. No relationship has any strength to it unless there is responsibility within it.

Therefore, the couple who feels that their life together is private and strictly their own, having no relationship or responsibility to and for all their other relationships, are two of the most self-centered people in the world.

Furthermore, their so-called love for one another will likely be intensely selfish. As we shall observe later, a true and strong love does not scorn the feelings of those outside a particular relationship or fail to heed responsibilities toward those surrounding the relationship, be it family or friends.

Instituted of God

Secondly, and most importantly, the marriage relationship, at any time and on all occasions, is held in the "preface" to be a high and holy one—"which is an honorable estate, instituted of God, signifying unto us the mystical union that is betwixt Christ and His Church." Marriage, far from being a casual or mediocre estate, is full of promise as well as pleasure. It cannot be treated as Janice, Carolyn and Bert did and still be honored. To honor a relationship is, simply, to hold it in the highest repute, or as one definition states it: "a relationship of profound respect mingled with love or devotion."

Marriage is a relationship set up by God, "instituted of God." It is not a mere biological arrangement. Nor did it simply jump out of the bushes during the early processes of evolution. To the Christian understanding, this relationship has all of the potentialities created by God Himself. It is not just a casual afterthought on God's part, but of the very nature of His creation. He planned and purposed it that way, though He is not the cause of our fracturing its potentialities; this we do ourselves. It is, again, a sin when the man-woman relationship settles for something less than what God planned for it and which He considered good.

And, most significantly of all, this relationship between a man and a woman is not unlike that between God and His people: "signifying unto us the mystical union that is betwixt Christ and His Church." This will bear fruitful examination in estimating Christianity's profound respect for the possibilities of this sacramental relationship. The wedding liturgy is saying at this point that the same kind of *devotion, self-giving, fidelity, sacrifice* and, yes, *passion* that were the essential characteristics of Christ's relationship to people are to be the same that mark the relationship between a man and a woman. Christianity, in this liturgy, could not more highly compliment the relationship than by making this pointed comparison! A couple are to extend to each other through mind, emotion and body a love like that which God bears to all His loved ones.

And these words are significant in themselves, for it takes devotion, self-giving, fidelity, sacrifice and passion to really make of a relationship something of inestimable worth. Without these Christ-related characteristics developing and operating between two persons, the relationship soon degenerates into a numbed mediocrity, the kind that God neither intends nor wants in the Christian estimation.

Devotion implies being consecrated to the other person, and this is something stronger than affection. Perhaps it may be meaningful to describe devotion as being an involved affection, not simply feelings for or about someone else, but feelings that are tied into the other person. In devotion we are bound together with one another.

Self-giving in the Christian sense is the kind of radical openness or vulnerableness that we have discussed. It is the freely chosen willingness to give of your self, of the very substance of your personality, to another. It is to extend, as a precious and unique gift, the person you truly are.

Fidelity is a rare commodity these days, but an essential to a man-woman relationship of any significance. It includes not only being trustful but also dependable. We can trust and depend upon how the other person stands with us, and we with him. Fidelity is the underpinning of a relationship, making it strong and, more important, secure. And a priceless security it is!

Sacrifice is often a difficult feat, more so in the Christian sense. For sacrifice in this context means a lot more than a grudging consent to give up something for the sake of someone else. To be genuine and therefore to be meaningful, sacrifice must be entered into willingly and seriously. An involuntary sacrifice, while it may be for good, is anemic in comparison to one entered into voluntarily, and it is the latter kind that gives not only quality of the highest sort to the relationship between Christ and people but which also gives abiding meaning and satisfaction to the fullest relationship between a man and a woman.

Lastly and most importantly, passion is to be a primary characteristic between a man and a woman. A disinterested or partially casual attitude toward each other hardly produces depth in relationship. Selecting some feelings to express and others to withhold or sublimate will not release the passion potential of a relationship. Passion is the freedom to express in their fullest one's joy, happiness and pleasure. It is also the freedom, a freedom sometimes neglected or forgotten, to express fear or anger or disappointment, for passion involves a lot more than positive feelings. The freedom to be able to express both positive and negative feelings with fervor is a priceless freedom indeed, although not without its own built-in difficulties; for anger that has turned to rage becomes destructive and captured in sin.

But freedom to communicate one's feelings, whatever they are, must be present. Harvey Cox, in *The Secular City*, points out how essential to a Christian understanding of relationship is the quality of being open, vulnerable, freely exposed and committed to the other person. In commenting on Karl Barth's phrase "co-humanity," which is his description of the basic relational form of man's life, Cox continues:

> This means that becoming fully human, in this case a human male, requires not having the other totally exposed to me and my purposes—while I remain uncommitted—but exposing myself to the risk of encounter with the other by reciprocal self-exposure. The story of man's refusal so to be exposed goes back to the story of Eden and is expressed by man's desire to control the other rather than to *be with* the other. It is basically the fear to be one's self, a lack of the "courage to be."[1]

Christianity's first concern is that man overcome the fear of being himself, and enter into all of his relationships, and not least his marital relationship, with the freedom to be devoted, self-giving, faithful, sacrificing and passionate.

Four Christian Affirmations About Sex

For all of these reasons it can be seen clearly and convincingly that Christianity does have a very high, and at the same time a very realistic, view of love and sex. Christianity could not conceivably place a higher value on love and love's sex than do these words of our liturgy. For the person who really cares, his love and sex are lifted high into "an honorable estate, instituted of God, signifying unto us the mystical union betwixt Christ and His Church."

We are now in a position to draw some conclusions, or affirmations, which are signally important to assessing Christianity's viewpoint relating to love and sex:

---

[1] Harvey Cox, *The Secular City* (New York: The Macmillan Company, 1965), p. 204.

(I) Christianity affirms the value and the pleasure associated with physical affection and sexual intercourse.

(II) Christianity affirms that sexual intercourse is a valid and valuable expression of the giving of one whole person to another whole person, by and through physical affection.

(III) Christianity affirms that because it is the *action* of *two* persons, it is to be entered into wholesomely, reverently, restrainedly, thoughtfully, considerately, passionately.

(IV) Christianity affirms that sexual intercourse is so profound an action of love that it likens it, potentially, to the relationship that exists "betwixt Christ and His Church."

Christianity, then, recognizes sex in love as a good gift of God, and not the source of evil, though it can often, quite often, be the occasion of evil (sin). Christianity's entire orientation to sex within love is why it prefers to describe a marital relationship as the sacrament of *holy matrimony*. While it is a distinctly human relationship, it bears all of the marks of God, of the holy. And Christianity would want for every man and woman these characteristics of relationship to be present and to be enlarged, rather than washed away by the manner in which man narrows down his capacity to love as well as lessens the greater joys of his sexuality. This is why, when a man and woman come together "in the sight of God and in the face of this company," there is great cause for celebration!

A CANDID VIEW
OF PREMARITAL
LOVE AND SEX

—————————— ⑥ ——————————

We will now draw as specifically as we can some meaningful and practical guidelines for premarital behavior. We have discussed the importance of the self, and *being* that self. We have discoursed on the meanings of love and the lively person-to-person tensions and problems in the development of a love relationship. And we have made four basic affirmations about love and sex in the name of mainstream Christianity. So it now becomes our task to apply all this to premarital love and sex. But we must preface such an endeavor by first focusing specifically on love-and-sex.

Sex Without Love

To have sex without love is to reduce the sexual capacity to the purely biological level. It is to shave off all of the many levels of personality that are engaged when two bodies meet in the intimacy of their sexuality. And this is to distort, if not permanently scar, the potential meanings of significant sexual expression. It produces dehumanization.

More than that, many young people are genuinely startled when, having sex without love, they find themselves disturbingly disappointed in the act itself. Of course it has its kicks, and it does provide a perhaps needed physical relief. But there is a lot more to sex than just the doing of it; and sex without love is not sufficient basis for a continuing relationship, not even a sexual one. Strange as it may sound, particularly to the ears of a young person like Cliff's pledge son, having sex *can* become a "bore and a chore" if there isn't something more to it than the sheer physical pleasure that two bodies can achieve with each other. And the personality suffers in the meantime. A person can be reduced to a state of Don Juanism, hoping desperately and certainly fancifully that his next act of love-making will be better and somehow more satisfying than the last one. But sex without love cannot endure.

Young people sense this truth, that love, whatever they mean by the word, has just got to be a part of it all. But sometimes this becomes a cover-up for a desire for sex without all the involvements that love adds to the situation. Many young men and women have to *force* themselves into thinking that they are in love in order to justify their sexual behavior. In our sex-saturated culture (Cox's phrase), seasoned as it is with the commercial investment involved in "romantic love," a young man or woman can go from one person to another justifying his or her sexual practices by being "truly in love . . . truly!"

Yet this is hardly the kind of love we have been describing on these pages; it is rather a fabricated excuse for people to follow their urges; it does justice to neither love *nor* sex. Moreover, if it is indeed self-illusion, then it is entirely possible that the participants' understanding of love and sex and their interpenetrating nature will be damaged to such an extent that they will not be able to have a normal and healthy love-sexual relationship ever in their lives. Many a young person prefers to think himself in love so that he can exercise his sexuality.

Love Without Sex

And there are always some who turn the equation around and approach love without sex. They feel that love is essentially ethereal, a vision into the breathtaking depths of an undifferentiated bliss. To such people extensive damage has been done long before they could function sexually. More often than not, and for a multiplicity of reasons, they have come to fear their sexual instincts and subsequently would divorce all notions of sex from their idea of love.

Or there are those who, rather than fearing sex, want to keep their love feelings unblemished and uncorrupted by their sexual urges. And if they can keep love and sex strictly separate, they can, in a way similar to those who have sex without love, have their sex in as free and corrupted a manner as they desire. They feel free to indulge with an unrestrained lustfulness that often takes on bizarre and orgiastic forms. They can love their girl or wife with a necessary amount of genteel sex, while having at the same time another relationship which is excessive and perhaps even lewd. Some homosexual behavior patterns fit into this group, but it is manifested heterosexually as well.

This leads us to a very central conclusion: *love is not only an attitude, but an action as well.* And we have come to the heart of the matter when we ask: *"What kind of an action?"*

Love in Action

Love and sex are inseparable unless they are torn apart and thereby dehumanized. Love is an attitude-in-action. We have suggested what love is in substance, especially as seen through Christian eyes, and summarized this toward the end of the last chapter. Now it remains to see how this kind of love behaves itself in concrete personal relationships.

What happens when love acts itself out, and what kind of an action is it?

There are four qualities manifest in love-in-action, specifically when acted out through sexual intercourse:

1. Intercourse is an act of personal union.
2. Intercourse is an act of intimacy.
3. Intercourse is an act of particularity.
4. Intercourse is an act of generosity.

1. An Act of Personal Union

Sexual intercourse is the action which creates a state of union between two people. They become in Pauline terminology "one flesh," and by that Paul meant the union of two persons—two total personalities—by means of the flesh. The state of union involves an acted-out commitment of not only one body to the other, but unavoidably one whole self to the other. It is an act of personal encounter, and cannot be less even if one or both persons intend it so.

There are two key words in describing sexual intercourse as an act of personal union: *indelible* and *intention*. First, inasmuch as physical affection and sexual intercourse are actions, they become a permanent part of each party's "personal history" and cannot be changed or undone. Intercourse is an act of union in which each person does something to the other, for good or for ill, which can never be obliterated. This is too seldom recognized, and becomes for some the source of guilt feelings which also cannot simply be erased.

Secondly, sexual intercourse, because it is an act of personal union, cannot help but affect the whole person and not just the body. By its very construct and nature, it draws the *whole* person into the action whether the participants intend to be so drawn or not. The very nature of sexual penetration and of orgasm cannot help but express a personal involvement and exposure of the whole person and thereby, unavoidably, some level of personal commitment.

Thus when one or both parties withhold or reserve in part the personal commitment which intercourse portends, their relationship is fraudulant, and guilt feelings arise. They didn't really mean what their actions were expressing. Their love was not of the calibre their actions indicated it to be. So love becomes dislocated from the sexual act, and the physical features of the act become paramount to the extent that the couple becomes increasingly sex-obsessed and the possibility of a love relationship in their sex life disintegrates and is lost. The sexual act of union is no longer unitive of personality. It becomes an egotistic and self-gratifying action which is finally dishonest, a fraud.

Sexual intercourse, being an act of personal union, involves the commitment of love whether genuinely intended or not. It belongs to a situation where full commitment consciously and intentionally can be made. This is the marital situation.

2. An Act of Intimacy

Tied in directly with sexual intercourse as an action of personal union is the assertion that it is an intense and comprehensive act of intimacy. We have described it earlier as the willingness or the freedom to be exposed and vulnerable. This is true on several levels. First, simply on the physical level. Sexual intercourse means sheer physical exposure. This is something man has been nervous about in some degree or another since the "days" of Eden. There is a real intimacy in being naked and exposed physically to one another, and it is not something we come by easily. Perhaps it is significant that so much, perhaps too much, love is made in the dark! But substantive love in action through sexual intercourse is free to enjoy the intimacy of physical exposure and pleasure, no longer intimidated or inhibited by being physically vulnerable (see chapter 7).

Yet the physical and sexual is only one of the levels of intimacy. Being an act of union, of intimate union, sexual intercourse brings together and blends the innermost parts of the two personalities. One becomes not only more intimately aware of the infinite number of personality facets of the other person, but he also becomes much more aware of himself as a person. He not only is willing to express to the other person things deep in his own secret world, but as they are touched and handled and loved by the other, he sees himself in a larger and more greatly defined light. In short, through the intimacy of union he is more free to be himself than he could ever have been in his solitary state. A man or woman comes into his or her own through the intimate and mutual exchange of which sexual intercourse is both symbol and substance. (Again, more in chapter 7.)

This comprehensive exchange of knowledge and of personality, freely offered, freely given, freely returned, gives a high quality of intimacy to the relationship, and sexual intercourse is the most specific and the most dramatic expression of this intimacy. Such a quality of intimacy demands the consistency and continuity of the marital state. It is not there for the asking, but develops only through permanent mutual commitment in the regularity and continuity of marriage.

3. An Act of Particularity

With human beings love always becomes quite pointed and particular: this boy who is sensitive and strong; this girl who is thoughtful and considerate. The kind of love we are talking about is not something that one sends out from himself to blanket the entire universe; deep love is not something that can be spread thin. In electing to give itself to another, love selects the person that will be its object.

To use a good, if old-fashioned, term, this is what courtship is meant to be: finding the person with whom we can be the most adequately comfortable. We do not, and cannot, lay all our innards on the table and let people sort through them at will. We would only be setting up an emotional cafeteria of our loves and our feelings, and no one can carry that one off. It would be nice to have everyone like and admire us; but, on second thought, we know that we ourselves are not able to care about every person we meet. We all have to have our defenses, hopefully healthy ones, in order not to be tossed to and fro by every human encounter.

Love is too precious and too tender a reality to extend deeply to more than a few people in an entire lifetime. We have neither the time nor the energy to compulsively love all mankind. We must pick and choose those few to whom we want to offer our affection, friendship and love, although this *will* overflow to many, many other people. And even then our capacity to expose ourselves and our love varies from moment to moment and from person to person however close they may be to us. Even in our most profound relationships there are times when we are less open and expressive of our care; this is only natural, for love is not an unchanging block of granite but an ever-varying, tender thing. Love has its loud and demonstrative moments; but it has its quiet and perhaps even lonely moments as well.

To extend a deep person-to-person love is difficult at times; certainly this is the case when it comes to male-female relationships: a man for his wife, a girl for her fiance. And sexual intercourse is one of the main ways in which love is demonstrated, be it violently or quietly. If this be true, then intercourse is intensely personal and necessarily particular. It is a couple's exclusive possession; it is by its nature not sharable with other men and women.

This is why young people who have "slept around" a lot before marriage come to expect too little of their sexuality, and even less of a warmly personal quality in their relationship. For many a marriage is primarily a domestic arrangement, and the greatest tragedy is that love itself becomes domesticated and lacks the rich and warm personal interchange that sexual intercourse was meant to give. These people have had so many indelible experiences with other sex partners that their married sex life becomes routinized very quickly, and the strong and passionate joys of mutual exchange on all levels, including intercourse itself, become dulled. A love that is not properly particular has defaulted in advance on the deeper possibilities of both personal union and intimacy. And because sexual intercourse, when it is the enactment of love, is a personal act of particularity, it needs to be enfolded in the commitment of the marital bond.

4. An Act of Generosity

The tug toward self-gratification in sexual intercourse is a strong one indeed. All of the physical senses are on the high alert before and during intercourse, and the desire to have one's physical needs met can be quite overwhelming. It is all too easy to forget about the other person entirely as we race to our own physical fulfillment. Sexual intercourse can be turned into as selfish an act as anyone is capable of, and the other person can become more emotionally distraught and perhaps even angrier than in any other situation. As we have said earlier, sex can be just as devisive as it can be unitive!

Therefore, sexual intercourse needs to be seen as an act of generosity. Instead of wildly submitting to the cravings of our own flesh, love-in-action through the means of sexual intercourse needs to be sensitive to the needs of the one we love, hard as that may sometimes be. And it does take time. Such sensitivity is not in operation by the end of the honeymoon, though the couple have been together both night and day, and likely not fully operative until the end of the first year of marriage. We have to learn first to see and then to meet the needs of our partner, and in so doing we meet more of our own needs. The knowledge that we have thoughtfully fulfilled the other person brings great satisfaction and fulfillment to ourselves; this is the reciprocity that is a structural part of a full and fulfilling sex life.

To grow in awareness of the needs of the one we love, our love needs to be expansive and generous. We need to be "on our toes" and ready to understand the startling complexities of not only our needs but also those of the other person, then to desire ungrudgingly to see to it that those needs are considerately met. The marvel of it is that consideration in kind will freely be returned. This growth in generosity takes insight, and insight takes time, lots of time, and the time most conducive to this growth comes within the regularity and continuity of the estate of marriage.

And So . . .

Taking a candid view of premarital sex practices, we would see that most, if not all, who have sex before marriage, however serious they may be, do not have much of a chance to partake of all the deep waters of love-in-action expressed through sexual intercourse. It is one thing to point to the damage and the dangers to personality that can come through premarital sexual experiences which lack the four kinds of action we have described. It is another to point out what young people are missing, perhaps permanently, when they choose to act out their "love" in a manner that does not include the presence of personal union, of intimacy, of particularity and of generosity.

It is short of impossible to tell young people what to do and what not to do. But we can point to what in the one case they are missing, and in the other, keeping. Finally it is their decision what to do with their personalities and their sexuality. It is there for the cheapening or the celebrating; and in this chapter we have sought for some of the conditions that would avoid the former and enhance the latter. These conditions provide an intelligent basis upon which young people can make their decisions.

AM I IN LOVE?

7

To love is to be human. Or to put it even more strongly and pointedly: to be human is to love. To live meaningfully and with luster is to be "in love." If we cannot love, we cannot live; our lives are reduced to existence only. If we have received little love in our lives, we have little to give and what there is will likely be none too healthy. Our capacity to give and receive love bears the scars of our early experiences. Few, however, are the people whose capacity for love cannot be brought into full play, genuinely and passionately.

Our stature as human beings is measured precisely by the range, the depth and the quality of our love. We are shaped by the *size* of our love. If we love but little, we are small. If the world we embrace with our love is narrow and shallow, we are shriveled. Without love we are nothing. The less our love and the weaker our love, the emptier we become, because we are increasingly detached and disengaged from life and reality. We are actually moving toward personal nothingness.

In short, perhaps the most despairing and devastating judgment that we can bring to bear upon any human being is to say that he *could not* love, or that he *did not* love. A person living in such a state feels unutterably empty, and this is hell, the hell of both the living and the dead.

Love is a relationship of attitude and action. On the one hand it is a yearning for the other person, a desire to be with and to participate in the life of the other person. It is a personal attraction, a lure, an aspiration, an adventure, a dedication. On the other hand love is a sensitive reaching out for the other, for his sake. It is a steady concern for his good. It seeks the well-being of the other.

One of the qualities of a genuine love is self-forgetfulness. This is not to be confused with the selflessness we have already rejected. To forget ourselves is to relinquish our self-preoccupations because of the presence and person of the one loved, and so be free to take the other person with a complete seriousness. Most of us at best exemplify ambiguous motivations in our relationships. For many of us, and for most of the time, our love becomes an enlargement of our own self-preoccupation and self-absorption: the other person exists *for our sake*; and this is very anemic love indeed, if love at all.

Some Criteria

"Am I in love?" That is a hard question, and often we are asking it in an emotionally charged situation. It is hard to think clearly when the heart is pulsing at top speed. Is there not some kind of structure or skeleton by which we can ascertain our feelings and make our decisions? Love must be seen on the highest level of responsibility, for, after all, *there are two human beings, not just one, involved!*

If we do not have some criteria for how much candy and cokes we consume, we will likely get fat and out of shape. If we do not have some structure of discipline in our study life, we risk the disaster of flunking. If we chronically arrive at work twenty minutes late, the chances are that we will not hold the job very long. Without guidelines by which to shape and structure our lives we would end up in chaos. And this is especially true in our love relationships, certainly so in the sexual aspects thereof. So we are going to make some suggestions, in the light of all that has been said thus far, for some thoughtful criteria. And what we have to say has a double application: *first*, to the nature of the relationship; and, *secondly*, to the act of sexual intercourse itself. This should be remembered throughout if these criteria are to have maximum usefulness, for we are, as we have said, dealing with both an attitude and an action: an attitude of love expressed in a physical and sexual action.

1. An Appropriate Action

Many of our expressions of love are inappropriate; that is, they do not fit the occasion. A person can ask for a physical and sexual expression of a love that is not present to the degree he professes, deceiving his partner into thinking there is a deeper quality to the relationship than in fact exists. Or, for that matter, for any number of reasons, the person professing the love may be deceiving himself.

William Hamilton, in his pamphlet "Faith, Sex, and Love," illustrates this matter of inappropriateness very well:

> If I had been introduced to you some months ago, and chanced to meet you in Grand Central Station later, what would be your reaction if I came up and warmly embraced you? . . . Among other things, you would be inclined to say that this embrace was an inappropriate symbol of our relationship. It was dishonest and inaccurate. It did not correctly indicate the nature of our relationship. By the same token, if I had spent 36 months in Korea away from my wife and on my return had knocked on the front door,

seen her open it and, extending my hand, remarked: "Madam, I'm charmed"—this also would be an inappropriate symbol of our relationship.[1]

A couple's physical and sexual actions are to be honest, accurate and fitting to the depth and the quality of their relationship. There will be feelings and actions that are touching and appropriate for a couple soon to be married that would not be so for another couple's second date. To express love inappropriately is simply a matter of dishonesty or carelessness that will soon make a relationship fraudulent. To care about another person is to be sensitive to what is truly appropriate to a relationship with him.

Hamilton contends that promiscuity is more often a sign of insecurity than of love. Premarital intercourse is reduced to taking one's personality-frustration out on sex. An insecure person finds *temporary* well-being by being the object of sexual love. He needs it to make him feel wanted and lovable, and perhaps even to feel at last mature. Promiscuity is not, then, a genuine and honest expression of one's self, but the assertion of an anxious person's will over someone else's body; it is far from a deep and appropriate gesture of love.

And when sex is entered into inappropriately it cannot be satisfying. Real needs are not being met, but actually are being exploited. It is for this reason that in most cases of premarital intercourse, as was the case with Janice, not only does disillusionment set in, but a basic hostility toward sex itself is instilled. And such hostility can be carried into a subsequent marriage, limiting the possibilities of that relationship and perhaps even doing it serious damage. On the other hand, a secure and healthy person does not have the

---

[1] William Hamilton, "Faith, Sex, and Love" (New York: National Student Council of the YMCA and YWCA, 1954), pp. 18 f.

need or the urge to *demand* intercourse with the person he loves. His needs for sexual expression are not diminished, but he controls his needs instead of being controlled by them, and he may well conclude that a particular relationship is of such a quality and depth that intercourse belongs, appropriately enough, to them only within marriage. To be thoughtful about the person loved is to do only that which is genuinely appropriate to their particular relationship at a particular time, and not letting one's insecurities cause an action which is more an expression of dishonesty than love.

2. A Non-Violating Action

Someone who truly cares will be consciously concerned that what he does and asks does not violate the other on any level: physically, sexually, mentally, emotionally, personally. To have intercourse with that person may well be to violate his or her personal identity. To have a considerable amount of petting may cause either person a great amount of physical discomfort, and that too would make the action a violation. When a person genuinely cares, the last thing he will want to do is *anything* that would violate the one loved; this can be a very meaningful criterion by which two people can gauge their actions.

There is a second dimension here as well. It is possible to violate oneself, one's own body or integrity or personality. And this self-damage, compromising one's self to do the expedient, can be painfully disappointing to the other person. We are loved because we are seen by others as someone of value, and when we violate ourselves we are also shrinking the estimation that others have of us; everybody suffers.

A second criterion for love in action, then, is the assiduous avoidance of anything that would splinter the personality of others or ourselves, be it physical, emotional or mental.

3. An Act of Respect

Tied in closely with the first two criteria for being in love is respect, a frequently overlooked aspect of any important relationship. Respect is love with honor. There was something good about the old days when people treated one another with high respect and courtesy. It was of course a style of life and manners, but in any event, it is an essential ingredient to any relationship. To respect others is to acknowledge their full dignity, to honor them for who and what they are.

It is impossible to love someone unless respect is indigenous to that love. And, again, this respect is many-sided: respect for the body, the intelligence, the personality, the person. It is to see and consciously enjoy the full nature and thrust of others for their own sakes. It is to honor their humanity and individuality, and all that constitutes.

Respect has that kind of seriousness. It refuses to try to make the other person over into someone else. Often men are guilty of being more concerned about what their girl wears than the person she is. A woman can be more concerned with the impression her guy makes, and the kind of future he can attain, than what makes him a valued and valuable person. This is only to disrespect the other person. If we cannot accept the other person as what he is, we have no business maintaining the relationship.

This acceptance does not mean that we condone everything the other does. But if we feel that we must make him over to suit ourselves, then something is disasterously missing in the relationship, and the whole matter needs to be reexamined.

The truth of the matter is that if a man truly desires to

change his ways, he will do it because other aspects of his personality are respected. No one changes out of pressure, or out of duty, at least not often. But people are more than willing to change if they know that they are loved and respected. For in that case a person may want to change or to mature, not because it was demanded but because he is loved with respect. A great many marital (and premarital!) difficulties would be avoided if respectful and respecting love animated the relationship. St. Paul talks about honoring all men. In this context, and with a special poignance here, honor and respect the one you love!

4. An Act of Communication

Communication? Easier said than done, at least on the level required by a love relationship of any substance. Communication between the two parties, freely entered into, is a *prerequisite* for love and sex. It is necessary just for the relationship to get underway. This is a strong assertion and needs elaboration.

The key word here is *freedom,* freedom to communicate the deepest feelings one has, and to receive the deepest feelings of the other person. We can use the word "intimacy" again here, recognizing that putting out our most intimate feelings makes us vulnerable. The criterion of communication therefore becomes: am I free to be *emotionally* and *physically* "in the raw" with the one I profess to love? Let us take up each one of these in turn.

Am I free to be emotionally "in the raw" with the person I contend I love? There are two sides to this too. First, am I comfortable in the presence of the other? Can I let down my hair, so to speak, and allow myself to be myself? Are there tender areas in my emotional make-up which would be better hidden than revealed? How free am I to be just my plain old self? Can I discuss those things about me which ache, which distress me at home or work or school? What about the things that tear me apart? How will my girl react to me if I am just myself, willing to communicate how I feel regardless of consequences?

Communication, authentic communication, rests on trust. Can I trust myself to be that self-revealing? Can I trust the other person with my innermost feelings? What will happen? What *could* happen? When we are free to trust someone else with our soft spots, or feel free to take the gamble, then it would seem that a significant kind of communication is present.

The second side of being emotionally "in the raw" is communication by listening. One of the beginnings of true love is found in the capacity to listen. But this, too, does not come naturally. Indeed it is far more difficult to listen than to talk. Most of us are full of advice for most any situation. We feel that we must always contribute something to the discussion, but no contribution of value can take place unless listening has gone before it. We forget, if we ever knew, that listening can be a greater service than speaking.

One of the greatest insights of the martyred Dietrich Bonhoeffer, in his book *Life Together* (Harper & Row, 1954), is about listening. He says that it is God's love for us that He not only gives us His word, but lends us His ear; it is God's work that we do when we learn to listen to one another. Listening does require learning; it is the perfected art of one in love. Many people are looking for an ear that will listen—genuinely, thoughtfully, empathetically listen— and with the couple in love, there needs to be an intimate listening. Bonhoeffer continues with his argument: he who can no longer listen to his brother will soon be no longer listening to God; he will be doing nothing more than prattling in the presence of God. Many a religious person who does not know how to listen, but only to talk, soon becomes a "religious chatter-box," rattling off pious words that *allege* concern and love, but do not *evidence* concern and love. One who cannot listen sensitively and patiently will soon be talking beside the point, and not really speaking to others. Such a person does not know how to love *because* he does not know how to listen. He is "talking the world to death!" Bonhoeffer concludes that anyone who is so preoccupied with his own ideas that he cannot listen soon will have no time for God *or* for his brothers, but only for a monologue with his own sterile ideas.

There is a further attribute to genuine listening. Like true love, it requires full attention; and this is hard work indeed. For instance, there is a kind of listening with half an ear that presumes to know already what the other person has to say. This is a common occurrence, but it should be seen as the presumptuousness it is. Part-time listening is really grossly arrogant.

There is still another kind of listening that is more editorial than attentive. It edits *in* the material it wants to hear and edits *out* the uncomfortable ideas and feelings of the other person. This is defensive listening, fearful of what might be said and the predicament it could produce.

To listen is to love, quite as much as is to speak intimately. To listen and to speak is communication "in the raw," emotionally speaking.

Regarding the second kind of communication "in the raw"—the physical and sexual—the situation is much the same. Physical affection and sexual intercourse are most intimate and inclusive ways of communication, or they can be. But, as with our emotions, it is not easy to be open and "in the raw" with our bodies, at least not instinctively. We are shy. We blush all over. We make love in the dark! Most married couples still do!

We need to be free to be comfortably nude physically as well as emotionally. If we can only be physical and sexual with one another in the dark, we are not free, nor are we fully communicating, for indeed our eyes and our sight are most profound ways of communication.

Communication, then, is a very complex thing, nothing so elementary as many people assume. These kinds of deep communication—"in the raw"—become a fourth criterion for love, one that needs development before the act of sexual intercourse becomes appropriate and fulfilling.

5. An Act of Discipline

Somehow a lot of people feel that discipline and passion are mutually exclusive. They hold that to be passionate is to let oneself really go. This may be true for the animal kingdom but it is more complicated with the human species. For with us sex is not merely the means of physical and sexual self-abandonment, nor simply of getting lost in the ecstatic climes of high passions.

For humans to enjoy fully their sexual life involves a considerable amount of discipline: not the kind that dulls passion but that enlarges and enhances it. This may sound unusual, but it is to make a double assertion:

a) The greater the control in love and sex, the greater the pleasure for both persons.

b) Similarly, the greater the thoughtfulness in love and sex, the greater the passion for both parties.

Discipline is love with muscle, even as respect is love with honor. A sense of discipline in love and sex ensures that the lover will behave in accordance with the nature of the other person. It ensures that that person will not be dealt with in a manner that suits simply our own mood or fancy, or in terms of our own whims, prejudices, misconceptions or ignorances. Only when we exercise discipline in taking care not to re-create the other person according to our own inclination can genuine love and successful sex be present.

The aim of discipline is to enable the lover to deal *justly* and *truly* with the other party, especially when he is disinclined to do so. We need the constraint, the control, which enables us to treat the other fairly. In short, discipline exists for the sake of love, and without it we get embroiled in distortions of both our needs and the needs of the other, and our whims dominate the relationship, setting it askew.

For these reasons, the greater self-control is exercised, the greater the possibility for full mutual pleasure. For self-control leaves us free to be genuinely thoughtful about the physical and sexual needs and patterns of the one loved; and the greater the thoughtfulness the more intense and satisfying our passions will be and become. An undisciplined love runs amuck over the other one, and is insensitive to the motives of one's own behavior. An undisciplined love, like an unrespectful love, plunges blindly forward; and this, interestingly enough, distracts from the height of passion that two human beings uniquely can attain.

The disciplined lover always has an eye for thoughtfulness and consideration not least in pre-sex and in intercourse, but, perhaps most important of all, *after* intercourse. Especially then it takes discipline to not go abruptly to sleep, ignoring one's partner at a moment so important. It takes discipline not to go wandering off with one's own sensations and pleasures. It takes discipline to be sufficiently forgetful of oneself to be attentive to the needs and the situation of the one loved.

So many of the searing disappointments about sex come about because love and sex and "passion" go undisciplined. Love without the muscle of discipline can quietly but quickly divide two persons, and oftentimes this can happen unwittingly, even unconsciously. The couple will discover one day that they are actually miles apart, and even harboring deep resentments for the kind of love that was more a matter of use than affection. Besides, nothing is more appreciated than attentive affection; it is one of the most precious gifts we can give. But it will not be there to give unless there exists discipline for the sake of love.

6. An Act of Joy

For many soon after the honeymoon, love and lovemaking can become more or less a routine chore. Or, for that matter, we do not have to be married to discover, as did Cliff, that sex is "not all it's cracked up to be." Sex is not just a capacity, nor is it even a skill. For human beings sex is ultimately an art. When it is approached as something less than an art, its potential for joy is drained away. Frequently for this very reason sex is especially disappointing to men as well as to women. To expect little is to get little, and if the primary reason for sex is to get a pleasurable physical thrill, and that is all, then it can rightly be asked if it was worth all the trouble. If sex is only, or even primarily, managing an orgasm, then a better case can be made for masturbation than for intercourse! Masturbation is less complicated. It is more immediate and direct. It does not depend upon a second party. It can have its own private fantasy undisturbed by reality. And it can guide the physical sensations exactly as desired. If sex is essentially coming to a sexual climax, masturbation is by far the winner!

While on this subject, we could recognize the current vogue among unmarried couples to indulge in mutual masturbation because they want for some reason to avoid sexual intercourse. This practice has highly unhealthy overtones. Certainly there is little skill, and no art, in this means of sexual gratification. But more than that, mutual masturbation has a set of sensations different from intercourse, and can most seriously dampen the sensations of intercourse at a later time. To be sure, mutual masturbation as a part of marriage and sexual intercourse can be an extremely meaningful and tender thing, but without them it serves to distort both the feelings and the expectations concerning intercourse. Any competent psychologist or psychiatrist can confirm and elaborate the significantly unhealthy aspect of mutual masturbation outside marriage.

But to return to love as an art, and as a means of great joy, let us compare love and sex to the work of a true artist. The artist may find considerable frustration in his effort. He may agonize over it, and seek to make it express all that he is hoping for and working for. But the final object of his art is the joy that it will give him and the world. Love and its sex are this way. The cup of true love overflows with great joy.

A measure or criterion, then, of love and sex is whether there is great pleasure and delight in the presence and in the actions of love with the other one. Or to use a good old-fashioned expression, when beatitude characterizes a couple's relationship they literally relish each other. They have more than a romantic tingling, though there is that. They see more than the sparkling eye when looking at each other, though there is that too. They experience an enfolding delight in being present and participating in an infinite number of ways with each other.

We find even a greater joy for ourselves when we are contributing to both the joy and enjoyment of the one we love. A joyful love is sportive, full of merriment. In short, a joyful love is playful, whether it is in sportively tickling the loved one's toes or tickling her fancy! A joyful love is one where the lovers are both seriously and physically enchanted with each other. Such a couple knows and experiences true rapture, not all of the time to be sure; but such joy with each other is one of the indispensable attitudes and actions of love and sex.

7. An Act of Liberation

This may appear to be a peculiar criterion to put here, but its place is fitting. Some young people get a good case of the jitters as their marriage day approaches. With some humor, and with some apprehension too, they talk about losing their freedom, and of the coming ball-and-chain of married life. And they may have a final fling with their freedom, often symbolized in the last bachelor party.

For some couples marriage is a prison, even if usually a self-imposed one. Two people can attempt to set up their own private world and go into hiding, but we might suspect that in such a case they *want* to hide and use each other to do so. Such a relationship is far from healthy; indeed it is enslaving.

A sound relationship is one that sets each person free. Love and sex are means, very special means, for liberation to a fuller expression of personality. It is impossible "to love oneself" in another person. Rather, through the intimacy of love and sex, we are more, not less, aware of ourselves and of what we care about and how we operate. And it should be so. Who and what we are, in good love and sex, is to be cared for and accepted; and we are consequently freer to accept ourselves as we actually are, and to be that!

If we love deeply, then we live extensively. We feel free to be "out in the world" with a sense of security and also a sense of caring for people "out there." In other words, a deep love overflows into other relationships, making them more solid and steady and meaningful. A couple's love which does not extend itself outside their relationship is suspect; it runs wholly counter to the nature of love.

This is quite specifically and naturally expressed in the way love and sex are tied up with child-bearing. The fruit of our love creates another life, a unique and precious one. Our love brings into the world another new person, and our marital love flows away from ourselves and out to that child. Our love for one another is set free to love still others. And our love, if it is a deep one, will almost at once set out to free that child to grow and mature, and finally to enable that person to give and receive mature love on his own.

The whole direction of love is outgoing, setting man free to be himself, able "to love and to cherish" his own life and those whom he would love. Therefore, if one's love and sex is of the kind that sets men and women free to be and to love even more profoundly, then this last criterion is significantly met.

There is, however, an additional side to this matter of liberation. Mature love is liberating for persons *as persons*. But it also liberates from the dehumanization of sex so prevalent in our secularized culture. Harvey Cox points to this:

> Positively it [preaching the gospel] entails protecting sex as a fully human activity against all the principalities and powers that seek to dehumanize it. In our day these include the forces, both within and without, that pervert sex into a merchandising technique, a means of self-aggrandizement, a weapon for rebelling against parents, a recreational pursuit, a way to gain entrance into the right clique, *or*—let the reader beware—a devotional act with some sort of religious significance.[1]

Culture these days strongly tends to crowd sex into one sort of technique or another, whether it is a how-to-do-it

---

[1] Cox, *op. cit.*, p. 213.

sex manual or the hottest pornographic novel. Sex is drenched with the impersonal, not least in that supposedly sexiest of all magazines, *Playboy*. It is not perhaps too strong to say that, from all corners of our modern culture, forces would emasculate the personal from the sexual, but at a price, for it is love that makes sex truly potent and it is the personal that makes sex truly profound.

A truly profound love and sex liberate us from these militant forces that would dehumanize both love and sex and leave us the ugly legacy of having sex, but without the personal, sex without its punch! Free to be our fullest selves, and free to have love and sex personally and profoundly whatever the rest of the world does: this is the last criterion for the question "Am I in love?"

WELL?
WHAT'LL IT BE?

In a very real sense each person's situation is unique, and it would be insulting to persons and to personality to corral everyone into a particular pen, insisting that they behave in a prescribed manner. It is the varieties of personality that cause us to be attracted to one person and not to another. We don't fall in love with femininity, but with a woman whose feminine qualities are particular and provocative to us. It is not the perfume she wears, though that does stimulate, and intentionally, but the personality that is exclusively hers which grasps our attention.

We have given some ideas about pre-marital sex and about the nature of person-to-person love. And even as we began with the situations of a Carolyn and a Bert and a Joany, we might perhaps benefit by reexamining them to see how they subsequently worked through their concerns. None of us will have exactly the same circumstances or the same experience, but we may be able to see their applicability in a specific and concrete situation. In other words, do the ideas and views presented herein work; do they have consequences? It is time to find out.

Janice

Here was a college girl who desperately wanted to be loved. Janice seriously doubted that someone, anyone, would care about loving her, and so she persuaded a young man to go to bed with her in order to prove to herself that she was lovable. After the experience she realized that she had not really cared about the boy at all; she hadn't wanted him for his own sake. She had simply wanted to find out if someone thought her attractive enough to make love to her so *she* might feel better about *herself*. She suffered great guilt, and no little despair, about the experience. She exclaimed to her roommate, "Now I simply hate myself!"

Some months, and considerable thought and conversations, have ensued since that time. Janice's thoughts now run something like this:

> It was an ugly experience. Ugly. Ugly! But it taught me a lot, though I'm afraid some of my classmates refuse to learn from similar experiences. It's a shame. Why must people my age have to prove so much to themselves? Poor Ken. It was a disillusioning experience for him too. I really hurt two people, not just myself. It didn't work; it never does. But thank God I learned something that grew out of it. I was fortunate though, because I confronted it head on.

> My problem was to accept myself as I am. This hasn't been too easy, inasmuch as I had built up so many depreciations of myself that I couldn't even see myself correctly. And I took it out on my body and on Ken, and it was nearly a calamity for us both. I see now what I was doing, and I also have a more accurate picture of myself. I wasn't nearly the inadequate person that I considered myself to be. I'm glad to

have shed some of the gunk which prevented me from seeing myself and accepting myself as I am. I'm so glad that Clyde came into the picture. He, too, has helped me understand myself, not only through our many conversations, but even more importantly by the way he treats me. He makes me feel like a woman, a woman he admires and respects; and this helps me to have more self-respect. I don't hate myself like I did—long before the "experience" with Ken. Boy, what a relief to be able to just be myself, not only to others but to myself as well. I feel like I'm living now, though it is absurd to think that all my long-standing problems have just disappeared. But I'm on my way, I'm alive now!

Janice has done a lot of growing up, much of which should have taken place earlier in her life. But most of us mature in fits and starts, some earlier and some later. We do indeed learn from experience, but assuredly we don't all have to learn the hard way. We don't necessarily have to create an unfortunate scene in order to learn and grow, nor will such a scene in any sense guarantee growth. We have already discussed the possibilities of permanent damage as the consequence, and it could have been so with Janice.

But grow we must, and one of the most basic elements of maturity is the capacity to accept ourselves mentally, emotionally and physically as we are, and not as we fear we might be. Acceptance of the self "as is" can be the basis of growing into the kind of person that we uniquely can become. It can start nowhere but in the soil of genuine self-acceptance, self "as is."

Eric and Marge

This serious couple raised the oft-heard question "Why wait until marriage?" They were in love and responsibly so.

They were committed to one another by engagement and planned to be married in a matter of months. And they had a slight degree of scorn for waiting until marriage for their sex life, when they saw couples who had the sanction of marriage actually more immoral in their relationship than they themselves conceivably ever could be.

They talked for several hours with their parson on two occasions. The three of them pondered thoroughly and thoughtfully the whole matter, and as a result Eric and Marge came to some conclusions of their own making.

They were looking forward eagerly to their life sexually with one another. They anticipated it not as something magical, but as a means of expressing their growing love and devotion to each other. In short, and on their own, they had a "high view" of their intended sexual relationship. They considered sex before marriage something that could be, at best, snatched for a few brief moments before they rushed back to the dormitory, and that would just not do. Or they could have a weekend in that small motel in a neighboring town, but a few hours or days would leave them only more frustrated when they returned to the regular routines of their school life which would not allow, by the very situation, the continuation of intimacy.

It would be all too unnatural. Sure, some solve it in this way, but it was not a solution, they felt, that was keenly responsible to and for the other person. For the kind of relationship that both of them intended, they began to see why sex needs the continuity and the consistency that comes only from *living* with one another, not for an hour or a day or so, but day in and day out, night in and night out. As strong as their sexual urges were, they spent a lot of time considering their responsibility to one another, and this raised the whole question of discipline—control—for them. They sensed that love and sex are not simply a series of sensations that transport one literally out of this world. Ecstacy, why yes! Rapture, yes! But is it the ecstacy and rapture of dogs or of humans, they asked. They saw that to maintain the marital relationship required discipline, that is, respectful control, a control that leads to greater passion and oneness. They realized with considerable insight that discipline was needed to make a marriage work, and work well. From this they concluded that it was entirely appropriate to have a discipline that took into account their sexual relationship before marriage, just as it would after marriage. They decided therefore not to grab their sex whenever and wherever they could, but to control their great sexual longings until they could "go all the way all the time."

Their parting words to their clergyman were: "We'll wait, Padre, and be glad for it!"

Bruce

Bruce was all caught up in the so-called "identity crisis." He was in a social climate, or felt he was, where he had to fit into the correct "image" and be and do what he thought his peers expected of him. He got irritated at times because his fraternity brothers all looked and acted alike, but he continued not to do anything about it. He did what he felt was necessary, and that was to maintain his mask like everyone else.

This continued well into his junior year, and he continued to "bed-hop," sleeping from one girl to the next in a short-lived but steady procession. Then there was a girl, Jill, that really caught his eye. She was natural; she was herself. He was greatly attracted to her, yet uncomfortable to an extreme in her presence. He began to realize that while she was able to be herself, he did not feel free to be himself.

About this time, his uncle visited the city where Bruce's college was located. And his uncle, the image par excellence, responded to Bruce directly and frankly. Their talk continued after dinner long into the night. Bruce pondered this conversation almost full-time for days, and his thoughts ran:

> Here was the man who always intimidated me. He almost smelled of the successful image-man, something I had to become but was afraid that I might not. The discovery of all discoveries (how did Euclid put it?)! He's a man! He's a person! He's not worried about images, hasn't thought about it in years. It wasn't *that* that made him the success he is. Have I ever been kidding myself. Such a—waste of time and energy (and money!) to make with the appearances.
>
> I have let "society" rape me into playing a role, pretending to be someone I'm not in order to get ahead socially, *and sexually!* I just want to be myself, and uncle has said it, *been it.* I want to be valued for what I am, and not least in bed! Bed-hopping has been an escape. I want to be known and loved for my own cruddy self. I must tell my Jill right now!

Bruce is a young man, like many, who deeply craves personal communication. He senses that life takes place when one can have moments of quiet intimacy with someone cared for. But up until now he has adhered rigidly to an image imposed upon him (both by his peers and by himself), and his sexual life has had only the appearance of intimacy. He has not been free to communicate the substance of himself to the girls he slept with, and, fearing that the real tug on him for intimacy might unmask his image, he simply went from girl to girl. Bruce was actually very lonely inside the facade of gregariousness and popularity. He took some pride, however thin he himself recognized it to be, in his reputation as the great lover on campus. Seducer he was, only to realize that it was he who had been seduced all along the way.

No, he could not blame his society; it wasn't so simple. He had submitted to the image. Yes, maybe, at least for awhile, he needed the image, the props. But, finally, his need—a much more legitimate one—for communication and for intimacy edged from under the mask of his loneliness. His uncle had helped him pull all this together, and to be free. How free? His words were, "I must tell my Jill right now!" Communication has begun!

Carolyn and Cliff

Carolyn had always been a sensualist, out for the thrills. From the time she was 13, her capers, her daring, seemed always to get her into some predicament. Her folks discounted it all, believing that this was a phase she had to pass through. Permissiveness was the way to handle it; after all, you've got to give kids a lot of elbow room if you expect them to grow up.

Carolyn had always wanted to experiment with sex, but she was somewhat fearful of it too. She didn't miss a sexy movie, and she spent hours consuming the latest love-and-movie monthlies. They were good for kicks, and, for that matter, safe. So by the time she hit her late teens, she had a picture of sexuality, and sexual intercourse in particular, that was distorted and exaggerated to an extreme.

Finally, she found both the occasion and the courage to enter into her first sexual experience. She felt she must go the whole way and experience the sheer delight of sexual orgasm. Her disappointment was blistering. She told her sis that she had cried solid for the following two days.

Carolyn eventually sought professional help, and in the several weeks of seeing her doctor regularly, she reached some decisive conclusions. One was to realize she had been trapped by her own urges and excesses. She had partially left the world of reality and lived in a world of her own fantasies. It wasn't for real. More than that she realized that she had reduced everything down to the physical and sexual. She had become a slave to her own body, and to its passions, or fantasies about its passions. As she talked this out with her psychologist, she began to shift her views not only about her body, but about her person. In one session she broke through by saying, "It takes more—a lot more, I'm sure—than two bodies to make a go of it." And, later, tears came to her eyes as she understood with a deep insight the doctor's remark: "Sex is a means of personal union with someone cared for. Sex is not a skill that two bodies coming together can accomplish. Oh, yes, on one level two bodies can make a strictly sexual go of it. Most anyone can reach an orgasm. But there is more to it than skill, than sexual prowess. Sex, finally, Carolyn, is an art, the art of love in which the subsidiary art of lovemaking finds its proper, and blissful, place."

Take Cliff. His attitude burned with the cynical. "Sex is not all it's cracked up to be. Sure, there's a quick thrill, but you have to go to so many troubles and preliminaries to get to it." So to his pledge son, he says, "Cool off!"

Cliff is inordinately selfish. He could be described as a first-class egomaniac. He can't be bothered with treating other persons, especially girls, with any consideration or thoughtfulness. He wants his sex without preliminaries, without any attention to the needs and desires of the girl involved. So he basically puts sex on the shelf, except when he must act out his purely physical needs, and then he takes what he needs and goes on his way. Of course, he is not exactly "humble" about mentioning to his fraternity brothers whom he has "made" this past weekend, for in his selfishness he likes to have the focus on himself. Cliff may change later in his life, or he may not. If he does not, his girl or his wife is greatly to be pitied.

Sally

Sally's anger toward her mother has long since abated. Parents have their problems too. She has thought a lot however about "the pill." It's unavoidable; several of her sorority sisters take them as casually as they do their vitamins.

She has come to the conclusion that for a lot of girls taking "the pill" allows them to shed responsibility for themselves. It provides an easy way to justify having sexual relations. "No danger any more, so why not?" And Sally feels that those girls, most of them, feel that they do not need to ask the question of the "personal" part of personal relationships. "Now sex is safe, so let's have sex." Some even use sex, within the safety of "the pill," to get their man. One very plump and unattractive girl got her first steady (and his as well) by seducing him, and to be sure, "the pill" is very important to them. Their relationship is quite sick, but well-supported by "the pill." As Sally noted, those two, far from being truly responsible to each other, are simply using each other by means of "the pill."

Sally knows full well that college girls' motives for using "the pill" vary greatly. Some are more healthy than others. But she has concluded that she has to depend upon herself and her own values about sex before marriage, and not upon a pill. "I intend to be master of my person, and not let 'the pill' and the reasons for its use master me and my passions."

Bert

Bert's father has calmed down after hearing that Bert's girl, Joany, is unquestionably pregnant, and his mother's tears are now dried. Bert is acutely mindful of how terribly he has hurt his parents, and Joany's too. As the four parents and the two young people sit together in the living room, trying to work out the situation in some responsible way, Bert sees from time to time streaks of utter pain spread across the face of Joany's mother. It causes him great pain as well. He realizes now with anguished clarity that what he and Joany were doing those past weeks in sleeping together was not simply their own business. Just look at the number of people whose lives have been put out of joint by what they had considered a matter between just the two of them.

As their discussion gets down to earnest, they see four possibilities. One is for Bert and Joany to get married as soon as possible, with the aid of the two families in setting up housekeeping, with Bert staying in school, and a good doctor for Joany. A second possibility is for Joany to bear the child, and through a reliable agency put it up for adoption. The third is for there to be no marriage, but for Joany's parents to legally adopt the child, allowing Joany to return to school and graduate, and start a new life. Or, fourth, Bert's family could take and raise the child in their home.

Although the tendency for these, as for most parents, is to have the couple get married at the earliest time, they do not run random into this solution. Two things have to be faced before this can legitimately become their choice. First, do Bert and Joany care enough about each other to want to be married and live together for a lifetime? They are still young and this certainly is not easily determined; but the question has to be asked, and answered. It would be folly, perhaps tragedy, for them to get married out of some noble sense of duty on Bert's part; that is no substitute for the possibility of a significant love relationship. Indeed if the possibility for love is not there, Bert might in later days use his "nobility" as a club to hold over Joany: "I got married to you for your sake, and you're indebted to me. Be grateful *and* do what I say." Getting married because the girl is pregnant is far from an obvious solution to their predicament.

The second consideration is the parents themselves. For their sake and for their reputations they might all too easily be drawn into encouraging the couple to get married. The parents too have needs operating in this situation. How will this reflect upon them, not least upon their fitness as good parents, if the situation is not quickly and, hopefully successfully, covered up? What will their neighbors, clergyman, boss, club, make of them as parents if this gets out? Bert's and Joany's parents discuss this openly and candidly. They know other parents who were so threatened by the possibility of the "news" getting out that they were willing to go to any length, any ridiculous length, to save face. It would be unworthy of them, as well as unfair to both Bert and Joany. With these things in mind, they list this possibility for the two young people.

Secondly and perhaps with more difficulty, for Joany to have the baby and place it for adoption is considered. Another set of parental needs at work is recognized here. After all, this is *their* grandchild that is being given one kind of future or another, and this is a potential trap to maintaining their good judgment. That good judgment must focus above all on the well-being of the child, on his or her best interests. The pressure is such that the child might be forgotten altogether, and none of them want this to happen despite the special or invested interest that each thinks he should have in the child Joany is carrying.

Then Joany herself. Her feelings toward the child in her body are particularly important. Child. *Her* child. *Her* child in *her* body. There is a whole constellation of emotions that are unique to a woman with child; these, too, must have a prime and sensitive consideration, a very tender consideration. Bert or his parents, or Joany's parents, cannot have the same set of feelings that are Joany's, and her feelings cannot be treated shabbily. Joany may not be able to exercise the best sense about the whole matter; her involvement, as it is for most unmarried mothers-to-be, is emotional in a way that the others cannot easily understand. Her feelings cannot be neglected or treated insensitively. Both sets of parents perceive this, and Bert also gets the pitch; but all admit that this only makes the situation more complicated.

The remaining two possibilities seem more remote, but deserve examination. What are the short- and long-range implications of either set of parents adopting and raising the forthcoming child? These two considerations are packed with even greater complications over the longer period of time. They leave open the possibility of greater guilt feelings upon the part of all, each in their own way. They also provide for a change of mind at a later point which could well put a potentially unbearable strain on all concerned, not least the growing child. These last two possibilities seem to be filled with all kinds of future difficulties, but all six of them feel that they too have to be fully considered.

The chimes on the mantle will sound many times this evening, and on evenings to follow as they ponder, as carefully as they can, what course should be followed, in the meantime collecting the kind of advice and information that will enable them to make the best possible choice for all concerned.

Well? What'll It Be?

We have tried to open up clearly and convincingly the issues of love, sex and faith. We sought to describe some of the meanings of being a person related deeply to other persons. We have focused on this in terms of love and the person, sex and the person, love and premarital sex and, finally, "what it takes" to be in love. All of this we have seen in the context of what it is to be a person, an honest-to-God self.

Our ending therefore must be *open-ended*. But this is not to be in the least arbitrary. Too much has been said to allow us to leave this open-ended in the sense of freedom to do as we please. We are indeed free, free in the liberty in which God in Christ has created us; and this freedom is not that of the libertine, of the Don Juan. Are such "personalities" free, or human? We suspect not, for their "personalities" show a great deal lacking when we give them more than a cursory appraisal. And we also suspect strongly that most young people want to take their personal relationships, and by all means, their physical and sexual relationships, as something of open (not hidden) value and worth.

Neat answers will not do for the issues of high living (in the best and correct sense of that word). Tightly defined specifications cannot be a substitute for thoughtful personal involvement between two people. Each person finally must come to some decisions about what he cares about and how this shapes his mores and behavior; and in the case of a love relationship, two persons must determine mutually what is appropriate and what is not, so that the growing quality of their relationship may be one in which each truly "loves, honors, and cherishes the other."

We underestimate young people when our basic presupposition is that they (perhaps we) do not have what it takes to act thoughtfully and responsibly in a given relationship, at a given time and place. Young people do want the advice of their elders, even when they feel sometimes that they should not let on that they do. And young people want, as well, some criteria for their conduct. Their parents also, for that matter, desire some criteria for their "adult" conduct, for age and experience far from answer all of the questions and predicaments of living! Young people, for the most part, are eager to take their place as first-class, full-time human beings—on their own, to be sure, but not without the feelings and experiences of those who are traveling the same basic route a few years ahead of them.

Live It Up!

So, once again, let us begin the celebration of love and of sex in love, with which these pages have been frankly, yet tenderly, concerned. Let us form our conduct in a way that honors both man and God. Let us be truly open to life and live it on all eight cylinders of our humanity. Love, and love's sex, is there for the joy of it or the ruin of it, or for the wonderful struggling for the very best of it.

A wise bishop at a confirmation service of two young men asked them to be seated as he had a few remarks to make. They ran:

> You young men have a few moments ago given your commitment to Christ and His Church. You have thought and prepared very hard for this oc-

casion, and it is far from a casual one for you both.
Rather, it is charged with not only great personal
meaning for you, but also places you in a long suc-
cession of people who have measured the quality
of their life together in the Person of Jesus Christ.
But there will be times when you will greatly doubt
what you have professed here today. There will be
other times when you will find yourself ashamed
and embarrassed by the profession you've made today. There will be occasions when you will be more
than ready to chuck the whole thing, for any number
of reasons. Let's face this now, not just when it does
happen later on.

But what I want to say to you now, and for
then, is that your life is now in Christ in a new way,
and of that life of yours I ask but one thing: Live
it up—*not down*—for Christ's sake.

How well those wise remarks apply to all that we have
said here. Indeed there will be times in even a thoughtful
and responsible relationship when the values we have subscribed to will seem doubtful. There will be other occasions
when our viewpoint about the personal, physical and
sexual will cause us embarrassment, perhaps even shame.
And there will be other, rather hot situations when we
will be on the edge of abandoning all that we considered
valuable to a worthwhile person-to-person relationship.
And those situations will come in many forms, before marriage and afterward as well; and they will be strong and
persuasive, attacking things that we have thought out carefully and treated preciously.

But this approach to love and sex we have professed
to be open-ended, and we are not about to compromise or

hedge on that. What has been given to us in love and sex, we are not about to take away. We will simply borrow the words of the bishop to say, in short, all that we have said before of love and love's sexuality:

Live it up—*not down*—for Christ's sake!

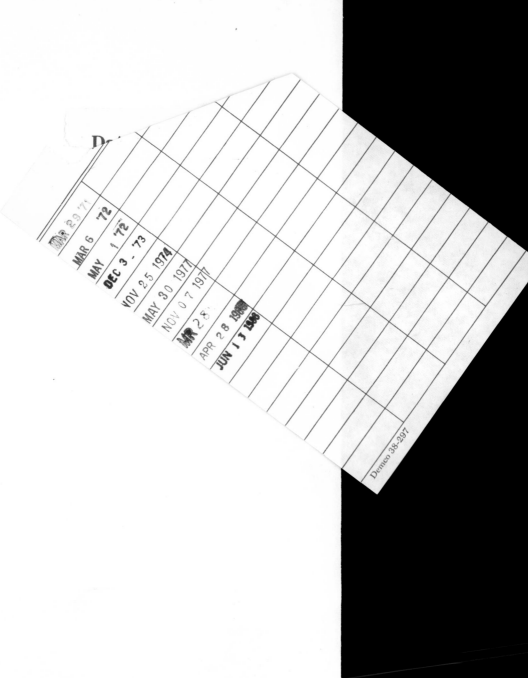